STORIES FROM WAGNER'S OPERAS

TOLD BY

GLADYS DAVIDSON

*The Flying
    Dutchman*

Tannhauser

Lohengrin

Tristan and Isolda

The Mastersingers

*The Nibelungs' Ring
(The Rhinegold
The Valkyrie
Siegfried
The Twilight of
the Gods)*

Parsifal

British Library Cataloguing-in-Publication Data
A catalogue record for this book is available from the
British Library

WAGNER

WAGNER

RICHARD WAGNER was born at Leipzig on 22nd May,
1813: died at Venice, 13th February, 1883. He was
educated at Dresden and Leipzig, where he also
studied music. Poetry was a passion with him as a
boy; and verse and play-writing occupied his mind
until a great enthusiasm for Beethoven turned it into
a musical direction. He was Musical Director at the
Magdeburg Theatre from 1834-36, Conductor at
Königsberg in 1836, Music Director at Riga in 1837-
39, and lived in Paris in 1839-42, where he struggled
in vain to obtain a footing. His opera *Rienzi* was produced at Dresden in 1842 with a success which obtained for him the post of Kapellmeister at the opera-
house there. *The Flying Dutchman* was produced
the following year at Dresden, and marked a new
epoch in his artistic history. *Tannhäuser*, the first
of his creations from the German myth-world, was
also produced at Dresden in 1845. After this he got
into pecuniary difficulties; and his sympathies also
being with the revolutionary movement of 1849, he
was proscribed, and escaped to Paris. By the efforts
of Liszt, *Lohengrin* was produced in 1850 at Weimar.
After ten years of exile, Wagner was pardoned, and
took up his residence at Munich, where King Ludwig
of Bavaria became his enthusiastic and generous
patron. *Tristan and Isolda* was produced at Munich
in 1865; and this genuine music-drama marked a
new epoch in operatic art. *Die Meistersinger* followed in 1868. Wagner was now world-famous, and
his colossal genius began to receive the support it
deserved. In 1872 his own great theatre at Bayreuth

was founded; and upon its completion in 1876, his noble tetralogy, *Der Ring des Nibelungen* was produced there. His last dramatic effort and crowning achievement, *Parsifal*, was produced at Bayreuth in 1882. Wagner's early years were full of struggle, opposition, and strife; but through all his disappointments he clung firmly to the new and great ideals of art he had formed, and in the end he conquered, his latter years being crowned with success and enthusiastic appreciation.

CONTENTS

THE FLYING DUTCHMAN

(*Der Fliegende Holländer*)

THERE was once a Dutch sea-captain who was so
brave and fearless that no amount of danger seemed
to daunt him. Battling with the wild winds and
waves was the greatest joy to him, and his light-
hearted daring carried him through many a difficult
passage.

But at last the crowning test of his courage came;
for, on a voyage round the coast of Africa, there
arose the most furious tempest that had ever been
known in those seas. All prudent seamen at once
sought refuge in harbours and sheltering bays, casting their anchors until the storm should abate; but
the Dutch captain only laughed at the fears of his
crew when they implored him to do likewise, and,
casting prudence to the winds, he swore that in
spite of the raging hurricane he would double the
Cape of Good Hope without delay, even if he kept
on sailing for ever.

Now it happened that this foolish vow was over-
heard by the Evil One, who was in the very heart of
the tempest, and, as a punishment for his vain boast,
he condemned the rash captain to sail the seas
until the Day of Judgment. The only hope of release
held out to him was to find a pure and lovely maiden
who would be willing to love him faithfully until
death; and for this purpose he was allowed to go on
shore once in every seven years to seek for such a
saviour.

Full of remorse and despair, the unhappy captain

began his ceaseless voyage, and the mad recklessness
of his speed soon won for him the name of the
"Flying Dutchman."

The fame of his terrible plight, and of the evil
influence surrounding him, became world-wide, and
all good sailors tried to avoid the doomed ship, cross-
ing themselves devoutly whenever its blood-red sails
and black masts appeared in sight.

Once in every seven years the Flying Dutchman
went on shore; but he always returned disappointed
and despairing, for no maiden could be found willing
to share his fate and to be loving and faithful to him
until death. And so, for years and centuries, the ill-
fated man sailed the seas unceasingly, and though he
daily courted death, yet death came not to him, and
every danger passed him by.

At length, after many hopeless centuries had gone
by, the Flying Dutchman steered his ship towards the
rugged coast of Norway; and as another seven years'
term was just now at an end, he determined to go
on shore and begin his hopeless quest once more.

By this time his vessel was laden with gold and
jewels gathered from the sea and coasts of many
lands; and by bestowing his treasures lavishly, he
knew he would soon gain acquaintance with someone.

As he drew near to the shores of a lonely bay, he
found a Norwegian vessel already there before him,
having sought shelter from a passing storm, and
presently he entered into conversation with the captain, and tried to make friends with him.

The Norwegian captain, whose name was Daland,
welcomed the stranger very kindly; and he told him
that he only waited in this dreary spot until the
storm abated, when he should eagerly make for his
home, a few miles further along the coast, where
his fair daughter was watching for his return.

When the Flying Dutchman heard that the Norwegian had a daughter, he was very glad; and presently he eagerly offered to Daland the whole of his

vast treasures, if he would give him in return a few
days' hospitality, and his daughter as a bride.

Now Daland, who was somewhat greedy of gold,
had long desired to find such a wealthy husband for
his beautiful daughter, and, though he knew nothing
of the stranger before him, and felt somewhat afraid
of his weird looks and mysterious crew, he could
not resist the desire to possess the wonderful treasures
described to him. So he gladly gave the Dutchman
permission to woo the maiden; and a short time
afterwards, the storm having passed away, the two
ships set sail for Daland's home.

In the meanwhile, the household of the Norwegian
captain had been eagerly awaiting his return for some
time, and on the day of his expected arrival, his fair
daughter, Senta, was spinning with her maidens in
the principal room of the house.

Dame Mary, the old nurse, was in charge of the
work, and under her directions the pretty maidens
were kept busily employed, singing merry songs to
the hum of their spinning-wheels.

Only one of the maidens was idle; and this was the
beautiful young mistress—Senta herself—who sat with
her hands folded, pensively gazing at a picture upon
the wall. The picture was a portrait of the Flying
Dutchman, who had been once seen by an artist
years ago, and whose story told in ballad and legend
was well known in Norway; and as Senta looked
upon that pale, sad face, a great pity for the poor
wanderer's terrible fate arose within her.

This face had such a wonderful fascination for the
tender maiden, that a great love and devotion grew
up in her heart for the tortured soul she longed to
comfort; and on this day of her father's return, she
gazed upon the picture with more intentness than
usual, for she had dreamed many times of late that
its subject stood before her as a real living lover.

But Dame Mary did not care to see her sweet young
mistress gaze so frequently upon the face of one whom
Satan had claimed for his own; and presently she

called out sharply to her: "Thou careless girl!
Wilt thou not spin?"

Then the other maidens begged her also to join
them in their spinning, and not to waste her sighs
and thoughts on one who could never be her lover;
but Senta said she was tired of the hum of spinning-
wheels, and asked Dame Mary to tell them again the
legend of the Flying Dutchman.

But Dame Mary would not do so; and then Senta
herself sang the whole ballad through from beginning
to end, in her sweet, soft voice.

She described the rash vow of the daring captain,
and the awful doom it had brought upon him, and
the song excited her to such passionate depths of pity
that, at the end of it, she stretched out her arms and
cried aloud, as though the spectral seaman himself
stood before her:

"I am the one who through her love will save thee!
Oh, may the Angels hither guide thee!
Through me, may new-found joy betide thee!"

As she uttered these wild words, which caused
Dame Mary and her maidens to cry out in horror, a
handsome young huntsman, named Erik, entered the
room, and heard all; and having loved the fair Senta
from childhood, and believed himself beloved in return, he rushed to her side in alarm, imploring her
not to forsake him.

He then announced that Daland's ship had just
arrived, accompanied by another and unknown vessel;
and when Dame Mary and the maidens had hastily
departed to set food ready for their master's welcome,
he turned again to Senta, and begged her to assure
him once more of her love, and to help him to gain
her father's consent to their marriage, knowing full
well that Daland desired a wealthier suitor for his
daughter than a poor huntsman.

The beautiful Senta only laughed at his doubts;
and when he reproached her with gazing so constantly at the picture on the wall, she declared it

was but pity that filled her heart for the subject of it.

But Erik was not satisfied, and he went on to describe a vision he had lately had, in which he had seen Senta give her hand to this very phantom captain, who embraced her rapturously, and led her to his vessel; and when Senta heard this, the glamour of her strange fascination came over her again, and she cried out wildly:

> "He seeks for me, and I for him!
> For him will I risk life and limb!"

Erik rushed away, wringing his hands with grief, feeling now that Senta must be under some strange and evil spell; and at this moment Daland entered the room with his mysterious guest, whom as yet he did not know to be the Flying Dutchman. He held out his arms lovingly, expecting his daughter to rush forward and embrace him as she had always done before on his return from sea; but Senta, with wide-open, intense eyes, was gazing fixedly beyond him at the stranger in the doorway.

There, in the living flesh, she beheld the face that had fascinated all her maiden days; and, spellbound with astonishment, she turned to embrace her father, as in a trance, saying: "My father, say, who is this stranger?"

Then Daland explained how he had met with the strange captain and taken pity on his loneliness; and he eagerly added:

> "Wilt thou, my child, accord our guest a friendly welcome?
> And wilt thou also let him share thy kindly heart?
> Give him thy hand, for bridegroom it is thine to call him!
> If thou but give consent, to-morrow his thou art.
> Look on these gems; look on the bracelets!
> To what he owns, trifles are these!
> Dost thou, my child, not long to have them?
> And all art thine, when thou art his!"

As he spoke, Daland, with the gleam of avarice in his eyes, spread out on a table the jewels and gold the Flying Dutchman had already given him from his treasure-laden ship; but seeing that Senta did not even glance at them, he thought it wiser to retire, and leave the stranger to plead his own cause.

When he had gone, the Flying Dutchman, with trembling hope, seized the hands of Senta and implored her to share his lonely fate, declaring that he had seen her in visions long ago, and believed her to be the one who should save him from his woes, and bring him peace and rest at last; and Senta, with rapture, consented to be his bride, telling him that she had also seen him in her dreams, and had longed to release him from his sorrows.

When the Flying Dutchman thus knew that Senta was acquainted with his sad story and willing to break the evil spell that had been cast upon him, he was transported with joy; and yet he nobly begged her to think of the sacrifice she was about to make by sharing his lot. To which the fair maiden replied heroically:

> " Him whom I choose, him I love only,
> And loving, e'en till death!
> Here is my hand! I will not rue!
> But e'en to death will I be true! "

At this moment Daland returned, and, full of joy at seeing that Senta was willing to accept the stranger he had chosen for her husband, he gladly joined their hands.

He then invited them to return with him to the shore; for it was always his custom, at the end of a voyage, to give a feast to the crew on board his ship.

When they arrived upon the shore, a gay scene was already taking place. Dame Mary and her merry maidens had brought food and wine on deck, and the jolly sailors were soon greeting their pretty sweethearts, and feasting, laughing, and singing with thankful hearts.

In strange contrast to this merriment, complete silence reigned on board the Flying Dutchman's ship, for though food and wine had also been brought out for the stranger's crew, they kept down below, and gave no sound of life at all. It was in vain that the maidens tried to attract their attention; and at length, alarmed at the strange looks of the silent vessel, they desisted altogether.

And then, when the Norwegian sailors, in their own enjoyment, had almost forgotten the presence of the strangers, the mysterious crew of the Flying Dutchman suddenly roused up and began to sing, in harsh, unearthly tones, a wild song, in which they told the story of their ill-fated master; and at the same time a dark, bluish flame gleamed around them, and loud rumblings of a storm were heard.

At first the startled Norwegians looked on in wonder, and tried to drown these weird sounds with their own gay singing; but after a while they grew alarmed, and, overcome by the dreadful scene, and full of horror, they hurriedly crossed themselves and retired to the cabin. On seeing this, the crew of the phantom ship burst into a peal of shrill, demoniacal laughter; and then the ghastly flame died slowly away, the stormy rumblings ceased, and silence reigned once more.

The Norwegians now knew that the dreaded and shunned Flying Dutchman and his evil crew from the abodes of darkness were in their midst; and Erik the Huntsman, shocked and horrified, rushed towards Senta, and implored her to renounce the stranger whose evil fate she had agreed to share. He passionately pleaded his own faithful love, begging her to accept it once again; and he reminded her of the old sweet days when she had been contented to love him, saying:

" Hast thou forgot that day when thou didst call me,
Call me to thee, yon pleasant vale within?
When, counting not what labour might befall me,
Fearless I climbed, gay flow'rs for thee to win?

Bethink thee, how, upon the headland standing,
We watched thy father from the shore depart,
He, ere we mark'd his gleaming sail expanding,
He bade thee trust my fond and faithful heart,
Why thrill'd my soul to feel my hand clasp'd in thine?
Say, was it not that it told me thou wert true? "

These tender, pleading words were heard by the Flying Dutchman, who was hovering near; and the wretched man, full of disappointment and despair, believing that Senta was about to renounce him, rushed on board his own ship and drew the anchor, crying out wildly: " Abandoned!   All is for ever lost!   Senta, farewell! "

But Senta, though torn by Erik's pleading, still found her love and devotion to the Flying Dutchman the strongest feeling in her heart; and, rushing forward to follow him, she cried:

" Canst thou doubt if I am faithful?
Unhappy!   What has blinded thee?
Oh stay!   The vow we made forsake not!
What I have promised, kept shall be! "

Erik, Daland, and others seized the distraught maiden as she fled, full of horror at the sacrifice she was about to make for one whose evil doom affrighted them; and whilst they held her back, the Flying Dutchman, though utterly bereft of hope, nobly vowed that he would release her from her promise to him, and sail away at once.

But Senta was determined to share the sad doom of the hero of her dreams, and by her faithful love to break the cruel spell that had bound him so long; and struggling until she freed herself from those who so vainly tried to hold her back, she ran forward to the edge of an overhanging cliff close by, stretching out her arms, and crying wildly to the hopeless figure on the departing vessel:

" Well do I know thee—Well do I know thy doom!
I knew thy face when I beheld thee first!
The end of thine affliction comes:
My love till death shall take thy curse away!
Here stand I, faithful, yea, till death! "

With these heroic words, the gentle, devoted maiden, in a transport of joy, cast herself into the sea; and, immediately afterwards, the phantom ship sank beneath the waves, which arose and receded again in a mighty whirlpool.

As the Norwegians gazed with awe and astonishment upon this wondrous sight, they saw, in the golden glow of the setting sun, two ethereal forms rising together from the sea over the wreck, and floating upward towards the heavens.

They were Senta and the Flying Dutchman, their arms entwined in a loving embrace, and a look of perfect peace and everlasting joy upon their radiant, upturned faces.

The ransom had been paid; and the Flying Dutchman was at rest for evermore, with the fair, sweet maiden who had loved him faithfully until death!

TANNHÄUSER

In the fair land of Thuringia there once dwelt a handsome and noble knight, named Henry of Tannhäuser, who was famed for his wonderful gift of song.

In a country where music was the delight of high and low, and where minstrelsy and knighthood went hand in hand, Tannhäuser was the sweetest minstrel of all; and when contests of song were held, it was he who most frequently carried off the wreath of victory. Nor were his brother-minstrels jealous of his power, for they loved him dearly, and gladly yielded him the palm.

The Landgrave, or ruling Prince of Thuringia, had a beautiful niece, the young Princess Elisabeth, whose gracious custom it was to bestow the prizes won at the Tournaments of Song; and, surrounded by her Court of fair maidens, she would listen with delight to the joyous strains of the minstrels.

But when Tannhäuser sounded his harp with the soft and tender touch that was his gift, and the notes of his sweet, wonderful voice rang forth, the heart of the royal maiden was thrilled through and through, and she grew to love the Minstrel Knight with her whole being. And Henry of Tannhäuser trembled when her fair hands placed the wreath upon his brow; for he also loved, and Elisabeth of Thuringia was the queen of his heart.

But, strange to say, so far from being made happy by his love, Tannhäuser gradually became very wretched indeed, for he grew discontented and weary of his life. Whether it was that he fancied Elisabeth

18

did not return his love, and that the royal maid would not be permitted to wed a humble knight; or whether an evil spirit tempted him, none can say. But day by day he grew more and more restless and heavy of heart—the joys, duties, and interests of earth no longer satisfying him—and he longed for a life of everlasting pleasure and delight, free from pain and trouble.

Now, in Thuringia, there was a mountain called the Hörselberg, or Hill of Venus, within which the heathen goddess of Love and Beauty dwelt with her Court, holding everlasting revels, and seeking to destroy the souls of erring men who fell into her toils; and in this evil, though enticing place, Tannhäuser (either despairing or woefully tempted) at last sought refuge from the griefs and disappointments of earth.

He vanished so suddenly and entirely that none knew whither he had gone; and though his friends and companions sought him long and lovingly, they could not find him.

And the Princess Elisabeth was so full of grief at his loss that she hid herself away in her own chamber to weep in secret; and though the minstrel knights still continued to hold their contests, she no longer graced the *fêtes* with her presence, but refused to give away the awards.

In the meantime, Tannhäuser was living a life of soft ease and voluptuous delight in the enthralling Court of Venus; and the beautiful goddess hoped that her loveliness and tender caresses were satisfying the wild longings of the handsome minstrel, whose soul she wished to destroy.

And for a time, indeed, the young man felt that he had at last found the peace and happiness he vainly sought; and the constant indulgence of his senses deadened his conscience, and made him forget that duty, labour, striving, and suffering are the only true means by which a man can attain to his highest level.

Thus, a year passed swiftly by in this abode of
monotonous joys and delights, where no count was
kept of days and seasons; and then, at last, a passing
return of his better nature came over Tannhäuser, and
he awoke, as if from a trance, to the knowledge that
a life of selfish pleasure cannot satisfy the longings of
a noble nature.

He was kneeling, at the time, beside the fair goddess, as she reclined on a couch within the glittering
cave where she held her Court; and on every side
were the sights and sounds that had enthralled him
so long.   A wide shining lake stretched out into the
distance, and in its rippling blue waters graceful
Naiads were disporting themselves, whilst Sirens of
wondrous beauty reclined on the mossy banks, their
sweet, silvery voices filling the air with enticing
songs.

Tender lovers, wrapped in ecstasy, were reclining
here and there; and in the centre of the cave a
number of dainty Nymphs were constantly dancing,
joined ever and anon by a train of wild Bacchantes,
who brought a whirl of tumult into their move-
ments, exciting all to a perfect frenzy of joy.

The sounds of music never ceased for a moment:
first low and tender, thrilling the heart, and then so
merry and joyous that none could refrain from dancing.   And over the whole dazzling scene a pall of
soft, rosy light was spread, gathering into a mist of
billowy clouds in the distance.

Fairest of the fair, and Queen of all this Love and
Beauty, Venus sat, enthroned for ever; and as Tannhäuser knelt at the feet of the goddess, with his head
sunk upon her knee, he felt for the moment that the
world was indeed well lost.

Then, suddenly, with this passing thought of the
earth he had left, the Minstrel Knight awakened from
his dream of bliss, and seemed to hear the silvery
chime of bells from the world outside, bringing back
to his remembrance the thought of fair things now
lost to him: the radiant sunshine of day, the starry

splendour of night, the renewing life and sweet verdure of spring, the nightingale's song of hope and promise, the delight of joy after sorrow, of light after darkness, that only mortals know.

In a flash he saw what an evil choice he had made, how cloying were the selfish delights that now held him captive; and weary of such monotonous joys, he longed to be in the world once more with its mingled joys and pains, understanding now that to strive with evil and conquer was a true heart's highest aim.

The deceptive veil of glamour was thus torn from his eyes; and full of remorse for the time he had already wasted, he implored the beautiful goddess for freedom to return to earth.

But Venus was angry when she heard his request, reproaching him with ingratitude, since she had found him despairing, and brought him comfort; and she begged him to touch his harp once more, and love her still, that all her delights might be his for ever.

Tannhäuser declared he would evermore sing her praises; but now determined to be set free from her enslaving toils, he again begged her to send him back into the world, saying:

> " 'Twas joy alone, a longing thirst for pleasure,
> That fill'd my heart, and darkened my desire:
> And thou, whose bounty gods alone can measure,
> Gav'st me, poor mortal, all its wealth to know.
> But while my sense thou hast enchanted,
> By thy great love my heart is daunted:
> A god alone can dwell in joy,
> To mortals frail, its blisses cloy.
> I would be swayed by pain and pleasure
> In Nature's sweet, alternate measure:
> I must away from thee, or die! "

Once more Venus poured forth her anger upon him, declaring that he slighted her love since the

charms he vaunted so soon wearied him; but the
Minstrel Knight replied:

" While I have life, alone my harp shall praise thee,
No meaner theme shall e'er my song inspire:
And yet, for earth, for earth I'm yearning!
'Tis freedom I must win, or die.
For freedom I can all defy,
To strife or glory forth I go,
Come life or death, come joy or woe.
No more in bondage will I sigh!
Oh queen, beloved goddess, let me fly! "

Then, when Venus saw that the cloying delights
she had to offer could no longer hold the awakened
soul of Tannhäuser, she at last granted his request,
and angrily bade him go back to the cold dull earth
once more, declaring that he would but meet with
scorn and disappointment, and be glad to return to
her sweet joys again. But the Minstrel Knight said
that he could never return to her, since repentance
and his hope of Heaven would now fill all his days;
and with these words he bade an everlasting farewell
to the lovely enchantress.

And then the dazzling Court of Venus suddenly
vanished from sight; and when Tannhäuser next
opened his eyes, he found himself in a beautiful
valley, between the forest-girt Hörselberg and the
royal castle.

Overhead, the radiant sun was shining brightly
in a cloudless sky, and on the mountain side a flock
of sheep were feeding, whilst from a rocky eminence
above, a joyous young shepherd piped a merry lay.
The fresh green grass was spangled with early flowers,
and the birds were singing in the budding trees; for
it was spring-time, and all the world seemed full of
praise and joy.

Overcome with gratitude, Tannhäuser sank upon
his knees to return thanks to Heaven for his release
from selfish pleasure; and humbly he resolved to lead
a new life of repentance and devotion.

Whilst he thus knelt in prayer, a band of pilgrims

on their way to Rome came by, and wound along
the mountain path, singing a hymn of confession and
repentance; and when they had gone, Tannhäuser
repeated the hymn upon his knees.

A short time afterwards, it happened that the Landgrave of Thuringia and his minstrel knights passed
through the valley on their return from a great forest-
hunt; and seeing the kneeling Knight, they drew
near to learn who he was, and whence he came.

But when Tannhäuser rose and faced them on their
approach, they recognised him at once as their long-
lost brother-minstrel, whom they had sought so
vainly; and receiving him joyfully, they eagerly
demanded of him where he had hidden himself so
long, begging him to return with them to the castle.

Tannhäuser replied that he had wandered far into
strange and distant realms in search of peace and rest,
which he had not found; and he declared he could
not rejoin their beloved ranks, since he had resolved
to lead the lonely pilgrim's life of devotion.

Then a noble young knight, named Wolfram, who
had been his dearest friend in the old days, stepped
forward, and said that the fair Princess Elisabeth still
mourned the absence of the favourite minstrel, whose
sweet music had filled her heart with love and rapture; and he added:

> " When thou in scorn hadst left us,
>   Her heart was closed to joy and song.
> Of her sweet presence she bereft us,
>   For thee in vain she wearied long.
> Oh, Minstrel bold, return and rest thee,
>   Once more awake thy joyous strain,
> Cast off the burden that oppress'd thee,
>   And her fair star will shine again ! "

The name of Elisabeth acted like a charm upon
Tannhäuser, for love of this sweet royal maid still
filled his whole heart, strengthened and deepened by
the struggles he had gone through; and learning thus
for certain that his love was returned, he flung
aside all thoughts of a pilgrim's life, and cried out

gladly: "What joy! What joy! Oh, guide my steps to her!"

The whole valley was by this time full of nobles and squires in hunting green; and when the Landgrave sounded his bugle, he was answered by a joyous peal from the merry huntsmen as they gathered round.

Then the brilliant cavalcade rode gaily forward with Tannhäuser in their midst, and when they reached the castle, high revels were held in honour of the Minstrel Knight's return. The chief of these revels was a grand Tournament of Song; and it was announced that the prize of the victor was to be the hand of the Princess Elisabeth, who, having learnt with joy of the return of Tannhäuser, had gladly agreed to be present, and to offer her hand as the reward, knowing full well who would gain it.

When the day of the contest arrived, the Landgrave, minstrels, and the whole Court assembled in the famous Hall of Song within the royal castle; and as the Princess Elisabeth entered with her train of fair maidens, she was received amongst them with great joy.

But Elisabeth had eyes for none other but Tannhäuser, who dropped on his knees before her; and raising him gently from the ground, she told him of the woe she had suffered during his absence, and of the joy she now felt at his return.

When Tannhäuser heard these gracious words, and knew that he might now win the hand of his dear Princess, he was full of happiness; and he told her that it was his great love that had always made his music so sweet in the old days.

And now the Landgrave announced that the theme of the contest was to be Nature and Praise of Love; and one by one the minstrel knights stepped forward to sing their songs.

The noble young Wolfram began the contest, and as he vainly loved the Princess Elisabeth with his whole heart, he addressed his song to her as a humble worshipper, whose only desire was to adore her from afar, and live and die in her service.

The other minstrels described the nature of their love in a similar strain; and then Tannhäuser sprang forward, and passionately disputed all that they had said. Having loved profanely himself, and being full of impatience at what he called their cold and timid hearts, he outraged the whole company by describing to them the voluptuous ideas of love he had gained from his sojourn in the Court of Venus; and led away by his exaltation, he addressed himself to the fair goddess herself, declaring that none but those who had enjoyed the enchantments of her embraces were worthy to speak of Love.

When his wild and beautiful song came to an end, a loud chorus of dismay and indignation arose from the company, and the minstrel knights, full of horror because one of their number had been in the Court of the heathen goddess, rushed upon Tannhäuser with drawn swords, uttering curses, and declaring that the gates of Heaven were now closed on him for ever.

But quick the beautiful Elisabeth sprang in front of her lover; and, though utterly crushed with disappointment at his unworthiness, she bade the knights stand back and refrain their curses and reproaches, since repentance was still left to the poor sinner.

The Landgrave now pronounced sentence of banishment upon Tannhäuser, but since Elisabeth had interceded for him, he declared hers to be the voice of Heaven, and held out one ray of hope. He commanded him to join the band of holy pilgrims now passing through the land on their way to the sacred shrine at Rome, and there, repentant and humble, to seek forgiveness from the Pope, not daring to return unless by him forgiven.

Elisabeth again besought her lover to repent, and set his thoughts alone on Heaven; and Tannhäuser, full of despair, seeing now that an illusion had blinded him, rushed off to join the ranks of the pilgrims, humbly praying as he went.

When the pilgrims had left the country, Elisabeth gave herself up entirely to heavenly thoughts and devotions, and every day went to kneel before a shrine at the foot of the mountain to pray that Heaven's forgiveness might come upon her lover, and that he might be restored to her.

Slowly and sadly the months went by; and at last the day came on which the pilgrims were expected to pass by on their return from Rome.

Early in the morning Elisabeth went to the Virgin's shrine in the valley to pray; and the faithful Wolfram, who loved her still in vain, kept watch on the path above, and nobly prayed Heaven to send the lovers a happy meeting.

At length a holy chant was heard in the distance, and soon afterwards the band of pilgrims came trooping down the mountain path and passed along the valley, singing joyous songs of thankfulness because their repentance had been accepted and their sins forgiven.

Wolfram and Elisabeth eagerly scanned the passing pilgrims with anxious eyes; but Tannhäuser was not amongst them.

Full of grief and disappointment, the royal maiden now resolved to leave the outside world, with its troubles and pains, and seek peace in the pure, calm life of a nun; and kneeling once more before the shrine, she solemnly consecrated herself to the Virgin in these beautiful words:

> " Oh, blessed Virgin, hear my prayer !
> Thou star of glory, look on me !
> Here in the dust I bend before thee,
> Now from this earth, oh set me free !
> Let me, a maiden pure and white,
> Enter into thy kingdom bright !
> In this hour, oh grant thy aid !
> Till thy eternal peace thou give me.
> I vow to live and die thy maid,
> And on thy bounty I will call,
> That heavenly grace on him may fall.''

Then Elisabeth arose in peace and returned to the Castle; but her heart was broken, and a few hours later she died in the arms of her weeping maidens.

When evening fell, Wolfram, sad at heart, stood alone on the mountain-side; and still thinking of his lost love, his voice presently broke forth into a low, sweet song.

> " Oh star of eve, thy tender beam
> Smiles on my spirit's troubled dream.
> From heart that ne'er its trust betrayed,
> Greet, when she passes, the peerless maid!
> Bear her beyond this vale of sorrow
> To fields of light that know no morrow."

The sound of the Minstrel's singing caused a crouching figure on the mountain path to draw nearer; and in this grief-stricken form, clad in a pilgrim's robe, Wolfram recognised the wretched Tannhäuser.

Still scorning his friend for having, as he supposed, deserted the pilgrims' ranks and never made the journey to Rome, Wolfram drew back; but when Tannhäuser assured him that he had indeed visited the sacred shrine, and returned uncomforted, he was filled with pity instead, and willingly listened to his sad tale.

Then Tannhäuser told him that, full of the humblest repentance, he had made the journey to Rome, gladly enduring more hardships and sufferings than any of the other pilgrims.

> " When I beheld a heavy burdened pilgrim,
> It seemed to me his load was all too light.
> And if he sought a pathway o'er the meadow,
> I trod, unshod, amid the rock and thorns.
> If he refreshed his lips by cooling fountains,
> The brazen sun poured on my head forlorn,
> When he besought the saints in murmur'd prayer,
> I shed my life-blood in the cause divine;
> When in the hospice he sought rest and shelter,
> On ice and snow it was that I sought mine! "

Amidst such hardships as these the poor pilgrim had at length reached Rome, and humbly kneeling before the sacred shrine, had begged the Pope to grant him Heaven's forgiveness.

But when the Pope had listened to his confession he said the sin was too great for pardon, and declared that it was as impossible for one who had dwelt in the evil Courts of Venus to hope for Heaven's forgiveness as it was for the rood in his hand to put forth green leaves.

And then, scorned by one and all, with his sin still unabsolved, and the hand of Elisabeth farther away from him than ever, the wretched Tannhäuser had followed in the wake of the homeward-bound pilgrims: and now, having finished his story, and being full of despair, he called wildly upon the goddess Venus to receive him into her dazzling Courts of Love once more.

In answer to his call, the sounds of enchanting music were distinctly heard in the distance, and in a thick, billowy mist that began to encircle the Hörselberg, the lovely form of Venus became dimly visible; but Wolfram implored the despairing Knight to refrain from again sharing these evil joys that would ruin his soul, and still to think only of repentance for his sin.

But Tannhäuser was hopeless, and felt that, scorned by the world, and denied to Heaven, the Court of Venus was the only haven left to him; and though he loathed the thought of its cloying pleasures, he was just about to yield to the enticing calls of the fair goddess, when another incident occurred.

At this moment, the solemn funeral procession of Elisabeth came slowly by, and passed along the mountain path, with mourning knights and weeping maidens singing a low requiem hymn; and at the same time, a fresh band of pilgrims appeared on the heights above and announced that a miracle had taken place on the night of Tannhäuser's departure

from Rome. The Pope's rood had put forth fresh
green leaves by morning light; and taking this as a
sign of Heaven's favour, he had sent messengers into
every part to proclaim that Tannhäuser's sin was
forgiven, and his repentance accepted.

Full of thankfulness that the prayers of Elisabeth,
now an angel in Heaven, had been thus answered,
Wolfram joined the pilgrims in their rejoicings for
the forgiven sinner, whilst Venus disappeared within
her mountain once more; but Tannhäuser, overcome
with joy, and filled with a wonderful peace, sank
dying beside the bier of his beloved one, and the
golden gates of Heaven were opened to him at last.

LOHENGRIN

During the early years of the tenth century, Henry the Fowler, King of Germany, gained great renown in all the countries of Europe, and by means of his courage and skill in warfare, had brought many fair cities and large tracts of land beneath his sway.

Amongst these countries was Brabant, over which he ruled as Liege Lord; and coming one day to Antwerp, the chief city of this fair land, to gather his faithful vassals together to help him to fight against the wild Hungarians, who had invaded his realms, he found them in a troubled state, since they were without a ruler, and their chiefs were quarrelling amongst each other.

Some years ago, the brave Duke of Brabant had died and left his two children in the charge of his nearest kinsman, Count Frederick of Telramund, who promised to love and guard them until they were old enough to rule the Dukedom for themselves. The boy, Gottfried, and his sister, Elsa, loved one another so dearly that they could not bear to be parted; but, happy though they were in each other's love, a great trouble fell upon them.

As the years went on, Frederick of Telramund came under the evil influence of a princess of another powerful family of Brabant, rivals for the throne with the late Duke. This Princess, whose name was Ortrud, was very unscrupulous, and a dealer in magic; and she had learnt the arts of sorcery so well that it was her delight to change people into the forms of animals, and to work all the mischief she could. She hated Elsa, who had now grown up to

be a sweet and beautiful maiden; and, determined
to bring trouble upon her, she persuaded Telramund,
with cunning words, that she herself was the rightful
ruler of Brabant, and that if he would marry her
they would rule the country together.

Now, Telramund wished to marry Elsa, whose hand
had been promised him by her father; but the pure
and lovely Elsa only felt scorn for him, knowing him
to be neither good nor worthy of her love. Then
Ortrud laid a wicked plot, by means of which she
hoped to gain her ends.

One day, when Elsa and Gottfried had gone into
the forest to walk and talk together according to their
usual custom, Ortrud, by her spells, caused them to
wander apart from each other; and then, by further
magic, she transformed Gottfried into a bird. Elsa
wandered about for some time, searching for her
brother, but at last returned to the palace, sad
and alone. Then the wicked Ortrud came forward
and declared that she had seen Elsa drown her
brother in the moat of a ruined castle in the forest;
and she soon persuaded Telramund that the maiden
had indeed murdered the young Gottfried. So Telramund renounced the hand of Elsa, and married
Ortrud instead; and very soon afterwards he claimed
the throne of Brabant.

The poor Princess Elsa was now very unhappy, full
of grief for the loss of the brother she had loved so
well, and in fear for her own safety; but one day she
was comforted by a vivid and beautiful dream as she
was praying to Heaven for help. In her dream she
saw a splendid Knight clad in silver armour, who
looked upon her with eyes of love, and spoke such
cheering words of hope that she no longer felt alone
and helpless. When she awoke, she spoke of the
noble Champion whom she now believed would come
to protect her; but Telramund and Ortrud laughed
with scorn, and declared this mysterious lover was
but the partner in her evil deed, with whom she
wished to share the throne,

It was just at this time that Henry the Fowler,
Liege Lord of Brabant, came to Antwerp to call for
aid from his vassals; and hearing of the strife that
was going on, he gathered the nobles together on the
banks of the river Scheldt, and declared he would
give judgment in the matter that very day.

When all the people were assembled on the river-
side, Frederick of Telramund came forward and
accused the Princess Elsa of having murdered her
brother in order to win the throne for herself; and
then the King called upon Elsa to defend the charge
made against her.

When the royal maiden appeared with her ladies,
pale and sad, she looked so fair and pure that all
the people felt her to be innocent; and as they gazed
upon her, almost with awe, she presently stood forth
and sang a beautiful song, describing the noble
Knight she had seen in her dream, whom she felt
would be her Champion.   These were the words she
sang:

" I saw in splendour shining, a Knight of glorious mien,
On me his eyes inclining with tranquil gaze serene;
A horn of gold around him, he leant upon his sword,
Thus when I erst espied him 'mid clouds of light he
     soared,
His words so low and tender brought life renewed to me;
My guardian, my defender, thou shalt my Champion
     be ! "

When the song came to an end, the King was so
struck with Elsa's angelic look that he declared so
evil a deed could never have been done by one whom
Heaven seemed to protect.

On hearing this, Telramund grew angry, and announcing that he had spoken the truth, he challenged
any man who doubted his word to fight with him.
The King now determined that Elsa's innocence or
guilt should thus be proved by single combat, and
calling upon her to name a champion who should
fight for her, he said that Heaven alone should decide
between them.   If *her* Champion gained the victory,

she should be declared innocent, but if Count Telramund overcame, they would know that she was guilty.

Elsa agreed to this, and said that her Champion
should be the noble Knight of her dream; and then
the King's herald blew a long, loud blast upon his
trumpet, and cried out: " Who will do battle for
Elsa of Brabant? "

There was a long, breathless pause, but no one
answered the call. Again the herald called out:
" Who will do battle for Elsa of Brabant? " Then
Elsa stretched out her arms and prayed Heaven to
send her the Champion she sought; and this time
the call was answered.

A great shout arose from the people, and all eyes
were turned towards the river; for there they saw,
drawn by a beautiful white swan, a skiff approaching,
in which stood a splendid Knight of glorious mien.
He was clad entirely in dazzling silver armour, with
a shining helmet upon his head, a golden horn at
his side, and a flashing sword girt around his waist;
and the beauty of his face and form, and the truth
and purity that shone in his eyes, were so wondrous
that everyone gazed upon him with speechless
wonder.

When the skiff drew near to the shore, the Knight
sprang lightly to the bank; but facing the river once
again, he uttered a few words of thanks and farewell
to the swan that had brought him thither:

> " I give thee thanks, my faithful swan!
> Turn thee, again and breast the tide,
> Return unto that land of dawn
> Where joyous we did long abide.
> Well thy appointed task is done;
> Farewell, my trusty swan! "

The swan then sailed away with the skiff in a
stately manner, and when it had vanished out of
sight, the Knight turned towards the amazed company
on the shore.

As Elsa saw him approaching towards her she was

filled with joy, for she knew him at once to be the radiant Knight of her dream, and when he declared that he had come to fight for her cause, she rapturously accepted him as her Champion, promising her hand as his reward should he gain the victory. The Knight of the Swan next begged of her to promise that she would never ask him to tell her his race and name, or whence he came, and Elsa already loved him so dearly that she gladly gave this promise.

Then the stranger drew his sword, and the fight began; and after a sharp conflict he felled Telramund to the ground, but generously spared his life. Ortrud shrieked with rage and dismay, but the rest of the company uttered loud shouts of joy.

The King now declared that since Heaven had given the victory to Elsa's Champion, the royal maiden's innocence was proved; and he commanded the people of Brabant to obey Elsa and her Knight as their rulers.

So Telramund and Ortrud were stripped of all their power, honours, and riches; and disgraced, poor, and wretched, they were driven from the palace, to wander in the streets as outcasts.

They could not, however, keep away from the scenes of their former splendour; and on the night before Elsa's marriage with the Knight of the Swan, they came, clad in their coarse garments, and crouched outside the walls of the palace. The sounds of revelry that came from within made them feel more wretched still, and Telramund began to reproach Ortrud bitterly for the trouble she had brought on them both by her wicked spells and false words.

But Ortrud answered: " List to me, and we may yet overcome Elsa and her Champion, and win back our power! Yonder Knight of the Swan bids the maiden never to ask his name and home. And why? Because if he becomes known he must return whence he came. Let us then put doubt in Elsa's heart by telling her he gained this victory by sorcery, and thus entice her to drag from him his secret. He is certainly helped by sorcery, and I have learnt by my own arts that if but one drop of blood be spilt of him to whom magic help is lent, all his powers will vanish. Do thou, then, seek to wound this Knight, and if I can also entice Elsa to ask his name and race, all shall yet be well with us."

Frederick of Telramund eagerly agreed to Ortrud's evil plans; and whilst they were thus talking together, Elsa herself, clad in flowing white garments, appeared on the balcony above, singing a glad song of thankfulness for the joy that was in her heart. Whilst she sang, Telramund crept quietly away, and when the sweet song came to an end, Ortrud came forth from her hiding-place, and called out: " Elsa! "

The royal maiden, who had thought herself quite alone, was surprised at hearing her name thus spoken; and when she recognised Ortrud in the square below, she was filled with pity at seeing her in such a sad plight. So when the wily Ortrud next began to relate a false story, declaring that she and her husband were under an evil spell when they accused her of having murdered her brother, and that they were now full of remorse and misery, Elsa's kind heart was touched; and presently she came down into the square and took Ortrud back into the palace with her, promising that next morning she would intercede for the two outcasts with her Champion Knight.

On the morrow, all in the palace were full of excitement and rejoicing, for this was Elsa's wedding day, and great preparations had been made to celebrate it in fitting style. Elsa was delighted at the prospect of happiness before her, but doubt of her brave Champion was already springing up in her heart, planted there by Ortrud. A fear that she would lose her lover began to fill her with dread, for her cunning enemy did not fail to point out that one to whom magic aid was lent might at any moment vanish from her sight.

When the bridal procession to the Minster was formed, Ortrud, clad once more in gorgeous garments, was amongst the train of ladies; but as they drew near to the church, her haughty spirit could no longer bear that Elsa should go before her, and angrily she commanded the bride to stand back, declaring that she herself should lead, since she was the rightful ruler of Brabant. Elsa stopped, full of surprise as she remembered how humble Ortrud had been the night before; and the angry sorceress now challenged her to name her Champion Knight, and to say from whence he obtained his mystic power and strength.

In the midst of this confusion, the King and his lords appeared on the scene with the bridegroom; and when the Knight of the Swan saw Elsa in conversation with the wicked Ortrud, he begged her not to be led to doubt him. As he spoke to her, Frederick of Telramund sprang out from a hiding-place close at hand, and, before all the bridal party, accused Elsa's Champion of having gained the victory over him by sorcery and evil spells, and called upon him to declare his name and place of abode if he would be regarded as a true knight.

But the Knight of the Swan still refused to tell his secret, declaring that Elsa alone could compel him to speak; and he added that the King and princes must be satisfied with having seen his deed of valour, and how Heaven had shown favour to him. The King and nobles now declared they were satisfied for him to remain unknown, and that they would always honour and stand by him for the deed he had done.

Having failed with this shaft, Telramund crept round to Elsa, and whispered to her the suggestion that she should allow him to wound her lover slightly, since, if but one drop of his blood could be spilled, he would lose his strange power and remain for ever at her side; and he added that that very night he would be near at hand to do the deed. But the Knight of the Swan came and drew Elsa quickly away, begging her to have no further doubt of him; and Elsa, gladly placing her hand in his, entered the Minster with him, and the bridal procession followed.

When the wedding ceremony was over, great revels were held in the palace; and ere these came to an end, Elsa and her husband were led to their bridal chamber by a splendid company of knights and ladies, who sang to them the following sweet marriage song:

> "Faithful and true we lead ye forth,
>   Where love triumphant shall crown ye with joy!
> Star of renown, flow'r of the earth,
> Blest be ye both, far from all life's annoy.
> Champion victorious, go thou before!
> Mirth's noisy revel ye have forsaken,
> Tender delights for you now awaken!
> Fragrant abode enshrine ye in bliss,
> Splendour and state in joy ye dismiss,
> Faithful and true, we lead ye forth!"

When at last they were left alone, the Knight of the Swan clasped his beautiful wife in his arms, and the two rejoiced together in their happy love. But joyous though she was, the seeds of doubt and fear in Elsa's heart, planted there by Ortrud, were growing fast; and when these first blissful moments were past, she begged her husband to reveal to her his secret, declaring that she would guard it well.

The Knight of the Swan begged her not to ask him, since all their happiness must thus come to an end, and he would be obliged to leave her; but Elsa declared that he was bound by a magic spell, and entreated him to tell her his secret, since she could not trust in him nor be sure that he would remain at her side.

Sorrowfully her husband again implored her not to question him; but Elsa, now torn with the fear of losing her beloved one, cried out wildly:

> "What magic can I borrow
> To bind thy heart to me?
> A spell is cast around thee,
> By magic thou art here;
> In vain thou wouldst assure me.
> Declare thy race and name!"

At this moment, Telramund, with four of his companions, broke into the room with drawn swords, intending to kill, or, at least, to wound the stranger Knight; but Elsa, quick to see the danger, handed her husband his sword, and with one blow of it, he felled Telramund to the ground, dead.

The noise of the scuffle soon brought the lords and ladies of the Court into the chamber, and the Knight of the Swan put the fainting Elsa into the charge of her maidens, declaring sadly that all their joy must now come to an end, for since she had demanded to be told his name and home, he must tell her, and his secret once known, he was compelled to depart.

So, as soon as daylight came, and the sun rose in the sky, the King, with Elsa and her husband and the nobles of Brabant, gathered together once more on the banks of the Scheldt. The nobles first of all gave their promise to Henry the Fowler to fight for him as faithful vassals against the Hungarians; and then the Knight of the Swan stepped forward to make himself known to them, declaring that since Elsa had asked to know his secret, he could no longer keep it from her.

He announced that he was a knight of the Holy Grail, and that so long as he remained unknown, he had wonderful powers of strength and might, and could overcome all evil; but once he became known to man he was compelled to depart and return to the Grail that sent him, for its Champion Knight must be guarded from all doubtings. He thus described the sacred relic which he and other pure and stainless knights served so faithfully:

" In distant land, by ways remote and hidden,
    There stands a burg that men call Montsalvat ;
  It holds a shrine, to the profane forbidden :
    More precious there is nought on earth than that :
  And thron'd in light it holds a Cup immortal,
    That whoso sees from earthly sin is cleansed ;
  'Twas borne by angels thro' the Heav'nly portal—
    Its coming hath a holy reign commenced.

Once ev'ry year a dove from Heaven descendeth,
To strengthen it anew for works of grace;
'Tis called the Grail! . . .''

As the people remained lost in astonishment at this wondrous tale, the Knight of the Swan added:

" Now mark, craft or disguise my soul disdaineth,
   The Grail sent me to right yon lady's name;
My father, Percival, gloriously reigneth,
   His Knight am I, and Lohengrin my name!"

As he spoke these words, a cry arose from the people: " The swan! The swan! Behold it comes!"

All eyes were turned towards the river; and there, in the distance, the skiff in which the Champion Knight had arrived was seen once more approaching, drawn by the beautiful swan. All this time Elsa had sat silent, pale and sad; but now she sprang up with a cry of grief, and clung to her husband with tears and entreaties.

But Lohengrin gently unwound her clinging arms, and sadly said:

" Too long I stay—I must obey the Grail!
   Oh, Elsa, think what joys thy doubts have ended!
      Couldst thou not trust in me for one short year?
   Then thy dear brother, whom the Grail defended,
      In life and honour thou hadst welcom'd here.
   If he returns, when our sweet ties are broken,
   This horn, this sword, and ring give him in token;
   This horn succour on battle-field shall send him,
      And with this sword he'll conquer ev'ry foe;
   This ring shall mind him who did most befriend him—
      Of me who saved thee from the depths of woe!"

He then embraced her tenderly, and bade her a gentle farewell. But as he moved towards the river-bank, Ortrud pressed forward and declared that the swan was in reality young Gottfried, the heir of Brabant, whom she had thus transformed by her magic; and she added triumphantly to Elsa that if she could have kept her Champion Knight by her side for one year, her brother would have been restored again.

But Lohengrin heard these words, though they were not intended to reach him, and sinking on his knees, he prayed for power to overcome Ortrud's magic. His prayer was graciously answered; for as the people gazed in wonder, the fair white Dove of the Holy Grail flew softly down and hovered over the skiff, whilst Lohengrin quickly loosened the golden chain that bound the swan. Instantly, the swan sank into the water, and presently there arose in its place the young prince, Gottfried, Elsa's brother.

Lohengrin led the fair youth forward, declaring him to be the rightful ruler of Brabant; and then, as the nobles were receiving Gottfried with surprise and delight, the stranger Knight stepped lightly into the skiff, and the white Dove, seizing the chain, began to draw it along.

Elsa, who had clasped Gottfried in her arms with great joy, now turned towards the river, and seeing Lohengrin standing up in the departing skiff signing a last sad farewell to her, she uttered a cry of grief and despair, and sank senseless to the ground.

Gottfried knelt in dismay beside her; and at that moment the Champion Knight of the Holy Grail vanished out of sight.

TRISTAN AND ISOLDA

In the glorious days of chivalry, when King Arthur and his knights were gaining honour and renown by their noble deeds, a stately barque might have been seen one golden noontide swiftly approaching the shores of Cornwall. Tristan, a valiant Cornish knight, far-famed for his prowess and untarnished honour, was bringing the beautiful Princess Isolda of Ireland as a bride for his uncle, King Mark, who held his Court at Tyntagel, in Cornwall; and as they drew near to their native shores, the ruddy sailors broke forth into a glad song of greeting, rejoicing at the safe conclusion of their honourable mission.

But there was no joy in the heart of Tristan, who stood at the helm, silent and full of gloom. For he, himself, loved this fair Princess of Ireland; but a dark blood-feud between them had forced him to stifle his own passion, and to secure her as a bride for another.

And a tumult was also raging in the heart of the proud Isolda, for she resented the alliance that had been made for her, and was filled with anger against the knight who came as ambassador to bear her away. For they had met before, these two, and a dread secret lay between them.

For many years there had been war between Ireland and Cornwall, and at last the King of Ireland had felt himself powerful enough to claim tribute from King Mark.

Morold, the cousin and lover of Isolda, was sent to levy the tax; but he met with a sorry reception.

For Tristan, the nephew and bravest knight of

King Mark, indignantly resented the claim, and challenged Morold to mortal combat on the shore; and, to his joy, he defeated and slew the Irish knight, whose head was sent back as the only tribute the subjects of King Mark would pay to Ireland.

But Tristan, himself, had also been grievously wounded by his adversary; and after searching in vain for a healer for his hurts, he crawled into a small boat and set it adrift in his feverish despair. The wind and waves bore the frail craft far out from the coast, and at last the wounded knight found himself cast upon the shores of Ireland.

Here he was hospitably received by the Irish King and his beautiful daughter, to whom he gave his name as Tantris; and the Princess Isolda, being greatly skilled in leech-craft, and famous for her knowledge of balsams and simples, set herself the task of healing the stranger's wounds. His noble appearance and pitiful plight soon won her heart, and Tristan, loving the fair princess directly he beheld her, was quick to vow fealty to her.

But one day, as Isolda sat watching beside the couch of her charge, she noticed in the sick man's discarded sword a curiously-shaped notch, which exactly fitted a splinter of steel that had been found imbedded in the skull of Morold, whose head had lately arrived from Cornwall as a ghastly token of defeat and defiance.

Knowing now that it was the world-renowned Tristan, the bold defier and enemy of Ireland, the slayer of her cousin and former lover, Morold, who lay before her, and whom she had nursed so tenderly, Isolda was filled with scorn and anger; and seizing the tell-tale sword in her hand, she rushed furiously forward, intending to plunge it in his heart. But Tristan's eyes met hers in such a pleading, helpless glance that the angry princess was quickly filled with pity, and felt she could not harm him as he lay thus in feebleness; and letting the sword drop gently to the ground, she crushed her revengeful feelings, and continued her nursing of the sick man. Yet Tristan did not dare to speak of love to her again, feeling that Isolda would now regard his slaying of Morold as a blood-feud and barrier between them; and as soon as his wounds were sufficiently healed, he returned to Cornwall.

Soon after this, peace was declared between the two countries; and as the crowning pledge of the truce, King Mark was persuaded by his knights to ask the hand of the Princess Isolda in marriage. Tristan joined heartily in pressing forward this plan; for, believing that Isolda was now lost to him, he felt that he could reward her best for her kindness to him by making her Queen of Cornwall.

But King Mark was growing old, and, being childless, had decided to make Tristan his heir: and it was not until his beloved nephew himself added his entreaties to the desires of the courtiers that he at length gave consent. Then, when peace and friendship had been sworn by both nations, and the King of Ireland had willingly agreed to bestow his daughter upon King Mark as the pledge of their truce, Tristan was despatched in a gilded barge to conduct the lovely bride to her new home.

Isolda submitted to her father's will with due filial obedience and reverence; but her heart was filled with scorn and hot anger against the brave knight she had nursed back to life and health. As she now reclined in her curtained recess within the stately vessel that bore her so swiftly away from her native land, she declared passionately to her attendant handmaid, Brangæna, that she had been betrayed by Tristan; for after vowing fealty to her in Ireland, he had but returned to demand her in marriage for his kinsman. Brangæna, alarmed at this outburst, attempted to sooth her mistress's angry feelings by assuring her that Sir Tristan had doubtless meant to show his gratitude by making her Queen of Cornwall; and she added that King Mark, though advancing in years, was good and noble in disposition, and worthy of admiration and regard.

But Isolda gazed impatiently beyond the curtains at the silent, motionless figure of Tristan, wondering sadly how she could support a loveless life so near that glorious knight, who now seemed so indifferent to her; for Tristan, struggling to repress the love in his heart, had kept sternly aloof from his fair charge throughout the voyage, fearing to trust himself in her presence. This seeming unkindness and studied coldness enraged the proud and unhappy princess to such a pitch that she determined they should die together before landing in Cornwall; and she sent Brangæna to the helm to command Tristan's immediate presence in her recess.

At first Tristan refused to leave the helm, remembering his duty and loyalty to his royal uncle; but when, just as they were approaching the shore, Isolda sent another message, imperiously declaring that she would not land in Cornwall unless he sought her pardon first, the trembling knight was forced to yield to her request.

Isolda meanwhile opened her casket of drugs and simples, saying she desired a potion that would cure her of all her woes; and selecting a phial containing a deadly poison, she bade Brangæna pour it out into a golden cup.

But Brangæna was horror-struck; and, determined to save her beloved mistress from the consequences of so rash a resolve, she poured away the poison, unseen by Isolda, and filled the golden cup instead with a love-philtre that the Queen of Ireland, skilled in sorcery, had placed in the casket for her daughter to drink with her husband on her wedding-night.

When Tristan appeared within the recess, Isolda began to pour forth bitter words of reproach upon him, declaring that though she had preserved his life when he lay in feebleness before her, she had still sworn vengeance upon him; and then, offering him the golden cup, she bade him drink its contents with

her as a final truce to all their strife. The ship was
by this time at the landing-stage, where King Mark
already stood with his lords, waiting to receive the
lovely bride; and, full of despair, Tristan took the
proffered cup and began to drink.

When he had swallowed half the draught, Isolda
snatched the goblet from his trembling hand, and
drank the remainder; and then the two stood and
gazed into each other's eyes in wonder and bewilder-
ment. For the strange potion was coursing wildly
through their veins like a fiery stream, changing all
their dull despair into the glow of passion, and filling
their hearts with uncontrollable love and desire for
each other; and at last, utterly powerless to fight
against the ecstasy within them, they fell into each
other's arms, overcome by a rapture they could not
quell.

Brangæna, terror-stricken at the dire result of her
fond deed, implored the lovers to recollect their duty
and the scene that was going on around them, for all
their lords and attendants were now waiting for
Tristan to conduct his royal charge to King Mark.

But the pair seemed wrapped in a sweet dream
from which the joyous cries of greeting gradually
awakened them; and then, when they realised what
had happened, they were filled with despair, and
Isolda sank back half-fainting into Tristan's outstretched arms.

But Brangæna, eager to prevent the immediate
discovery of their hapless love, quickly roused her
mistress, and hung upon her shoulders the gorgeous
royal mantle that had been provided for her nuptials;
and then Tristan, as in a trance, with woe in his
heart, led his beloved one forth from the ship, and
delivered her into the hands of his Sovereign.

Isolda and King Mark were immediately wedded,
amidst great rejoicings; but although the unhappy
victims of the fatal love-potion had strength to loyally
fulfil this pledge of peace between the two countries,
they could not long keep their devouring passion

within bounds. With the help of the devoted and remorseful Brangæna, they frequently met in secret, and the rapture of these stolen interviews was as balm to their bleeding hearts, the one sweet chain that kept them still bound to life.

But Tristan had an enemy, a knight named Melot, who, under the disguise of friendship, had gained his confidence and learnt the secret of his hopeless passion, and who, having no real love for the man he called his friend, determined to use this woeful secret for his own base ends. For Melot was jealous of the renown and noble qualities of Tristan, and longed to supplant him in the regard of his royal master; and having now discovered a weapon to his hand in the secret confided to him by the unsuspecting knight, he eagerly sought an opportunity for betraying him, and quickly found one.

Having persuaded the King to arrange a royal hunt one beautiful summer night, the crafty Melot easily induced Tristan to remain behind, and so secure a long, sweet interview with his beloved Isolda; but the false friend gaily joined in the chase, intending to return in a short time with the King to entrap the lovers.

When the hunting party had departed into the depths of the forest, and the merry sounds of the horns could only be heard in the far distance, Isolda crept forth from the silent castle, followed by her faithful handmaid; and bidding Brangæna keep watch near the forest, she flung a lighted torch to the ground, this being the signal for Tristan's approach. She then ran down the steps towards a moon-lit avenue, and in another moment the lovers were clasped in each other's arms.

It was a moment of intense joy; and as the enraptured pair reclined together upon a mossy bank studded with sleeping flowers, they poured out to each other, in tenderest phrases, the passionate love they were compelled to keep pent within their hearts before the eyes of the world. It was midnight; but the happy lovers cared naught for time, and would gladly have remained in such sweet converse for ever.

But suddenly there was a cry from Brangæna, who rushed wildly forward, declaring that they were betrayed; and next moment, King Mark and a few of his lords broke hastily into the avenue, having been led to the spot by Melot, who had found an opportunity during the hunt to inform his royal master of the lovers' intended meeting.

At first King Mark had refused to believe that his noblest and best-beloved knight could thus betray his honour; but as he stepped into the avenue, and the living proof of it met his gaze, he was filled with deepest grief, and began to pour forth bitter reproaches upon the wretched Tristan, who vainly endeavoured to hide Isolda's shrinking form from the scornful gaze of the courtiers.

Stung by the just reproaches of the King, and enraged at the cruel treachery of his false friend, Tristan drew his sword and challenged Melot to fight; and in his despair, caring little to defend himself, he allowed his adversary to overcome him, and soon fell to the ground mortally wounded.

Isolda was borne back fainting to the castle, followed by King Mark and his courtiers; and Tristan was carried, in a dying condition, on board a vessel by his faithful henchman, Kurvenal, who quickly set sail for Brittany, where his master owned a castle overlooking the sea.

Here the sick man was at length placed in safety by Kurvenal, who endeavoured to restore him to health; but finding that his beloved master's wounds were too serious for him to heal, and that he grew worse instead of better, the poor henchman was in despair. At last he bethought him to send for Isolda herself, whom he knew to be greatly skilled in leechcraft; and thinking only of his master's physical needs, he despatched a messenger in a swift vessel, to entreat the beautiful Queen to come and heal her almost dying lover.

For several days after, Tristan remained in an unconscious state; but upon being brought out into an open courtyard one sunny noontide, he awoke from his torpor, and feebly asked for Isolda. Kurvenal answered that he had sent for her to come with healing balsams for his wounds; and, running to the walls, he exclaimed joyfully that the vessel was even now returning with Isolda on board.

Tristan was overjoyed at this glad news, and when Kurvenal presently went to receive the welcome guest at the castle gates, the wounded man's excitement knew no bounds. In his eagerness to see his beloved one once again, he endeavoured to crawl from the couch; but the effort of moving caused his terrible wounds to open afresh, and just as Isolda rushed through the gateway, he uttered her name with a gasping cry of joy, and fell back dead upon the couch.

Isolda, with a loud shriek of woe, fell fainting upon his prostrate body, and at that moment Kurvenal was hailed by a second vessel that had immediately followed in the wake of the first. On this barque were King Mark with his knights, and also Brangæna; and quickly surmising that they were come with hostile intentions, the brave henchman barricaded the entrance to the castle, and refused admittance to the newcomers, who had instantly landed.

Then when the eager knights, by their superior force, broke through the gateway, Kurvenal sprang furiously upon them and fought desperately, in spite of their cries that they came in peace. The first to enter was the traitor, Melot, and with a cry of triumph, Kurvenal thrust him through the heart. Then receiving a mortal wound himself, the faithful henchman crawled to the couch of the dead Tristan, and feeling for his beloved master's hand, he sank, dying, at his feet.

King Mark and his party now rushed forward, unhindered; and Brangæna, raising her still breathing mistress in her arms, besought her to revive, since

she had come with good news for her. For upon
the flight of Isolda to the aid of Tristan, Brangæna
had, in desperation, sought King Mark, and told him
of how, quite unconsciously, Tristan and Isolda had
swallowed the magic potion that had made them
lovers for life; and, rejoicing to learn that his best-
loved knight and beautiful Queen were thus free from
blame, since they were powerless to fight against the
mighty philtre, the noble-hearted King was filled with
pity for the sufferings they had endured. He resolved
generously to renounce Isolda, and permit the unhappy lovers to be united; and immediately entering
his ship, he had followed with Brangæna and his
knights in the wake of the flying Queen.

But the vessel had arrived too late, for Tristan was
already dead; and full of grief, King Mark knelt,
weeping, at the foot of the couch. And it was in
vain that Brangæna tried to raise the quivering form
of her beloved mistress; for Isolda's heart was broken,
and with a last despairing cry, she fell back lifeless to
the ground.

Thus had the magic philtre wrought destruction;
and in death only were the lovers united.

D.

THE MASTERSINGERS OF NUREMBERG

(Die Meistersinger von Nürnberg)

AFTER the decay of the knightly court poetry of the
Minnesingers, whose pure and noble art had been
inspired and encouraged by the age of chivalry in
which they lived, the spontaneous love of song,
natural to the character of the German people, was
lost for a time in the gloom and ignorance of the
dark Middle Ages; but, later on, when the Reforma-
tion had once more lighted the way to knowledge
and culture, the beautiful art was revived by guilds
of musical enthusiasts, known as The Mastersingers.

But the dramatic, chivalric conception of life,
which had been the prevailing spirit of the Minnesingers of old, all of whom had been of noble birth
and exercised their art in the courts of kings, never
quite returned; for the Mastersingers, being but
humble burghers and artisans, could not attain to
such courtly grace of expression, and their art was
naturally of a stiffer and more pedantic character.
Yet they did excellent work, establishing schools
and guilds of poetry and song in most of the principal towns of Germany; but by hedging themselves
in by narrow rules and conventions, they left little
margin for the soaring spirit of true genius, which
ever chafes at petty restraints, and insists on freedom
of fancy.

In Nuremberg, the Mastersingers attained to the
greatest excellence of their class; and in the middle
of the sixteenth century there flourished in this
community, the simple-minded, large-hearted Hans

Sachs, the truest poet of his time, whose broad views were in refreshing contrast to the dull and cramped conceptions of art held by most of the Mastersingers.

It was during the time when Hans Sachs was a leader amongst the celebrated Mastersingers of Nuremberg, that this story opens; and upon St. John's Eve in a certain year, he and his musical friends were called upon to undergo a new and exciting experience in the pursuit of their beloved art.

Veit Pogner, a goldsmith, and the wealthiest of the older Mastersingers, impelled by an enthusiastic love of art, had just offered the hand of his beautiful daughter, Eva, together with the inheritance of all his riches and worldly possessions, as a prize to the master musician who should gain the wreath of victory in the grand contest to be held on St. John's Day, in accordance with the usual custom.

Amongst the competing masters who felt most confident of success was Sixtus Beckmesser, the town clerk, who occupied the important office of marker in the society, an officer whose duty it was to mark on a slate the faults made against the established rules and regulations of the Guild. Beckmesser, though without talent, and no longer young, nor even possessed of any pleasing personal charms, was so conceited that he fancied none to be his equal in music and poetry; and in spite of the fact that Eva was to have power to refuse the prize-winner, should he prove distasteful to her, he yet felt assured of success, though the maiden had never shown signs of favour to him.

As a matter of fact, Eva had already fixed her affections upon a young knight, one Sir Walter von Stolzing, who, being descended from the old Minne-singers, whose glorious achievements he had read of and studied, and in whom the truly poetic, romantic, and knightly art was revived, had left his now de-caying ancestral hall, in order to find kindred spirits amongst the celebrated Mastersingers of music-loving Nuremberg; and having once been brought into contact with the soaring, enthusiastic spirit of this noble youth, she could never again be contented with the pedantic methods of the burgher Mastersingers.

Walter, having business relations with old Pogner in connection with his poverty-stricken estate, had thus made acquaintance with the goldsmith's fair daughter; and the exquisite soul-inspiring beauty and pure, sweet nature of this maiden having quickly kindled a consuming passion in his impetuous, romantic heart, and knowing that his love was returned, he determined to enter the ranks of the competitors on St. John's Day, since none but a Mastersinger could aspire to her hand, and trusted that his great love would enable his song to gain the victor's wreath.

For this reason, he repaired on St. John's Eve to the Church of St. Katherine, where the Mastersingers held their meetings, and requested to be admitted to the competition. He was greatly disconcerted on being informed by a lively young man named David, who was apprenticed to Hans Sachs the cobbler, that the musical guild was arranged as a trades' guild, with degrees of membership, such as apprentices, scholars, and singers, and that it was usual to spend at least a year in each degree before attaining to the rank of a " master "; and he was filled with impatience on hearing of the many petty rules and narrow restrictions in verse and song-making which were necessary to be observed ere he could hope to please the Mastersingers, who had absolute faith in their own standard of perfection, and refused to admit into their ranks any who failed to conform to the same, seven faults only against the rules being allowed to candidates for admission to their competitions.

Nevertheless, still believing in his own natural gifts, which he had cultivated in the beautiful woodlands of his birthplace, untrammelled by forms and conventions, when the Mastersingers had assembled, he requested permission to prove to them that he was a master of poetic song, and therefore justified in entering the competition on the morrow; and, since he was introduced to them by Pogner himself, who vouched for his good faith, he was invited to sing a song, though the Guild members were horrified on hearing that he had never studied in any Mastersinging guild, and had received no other instruction than that afforded by a love of Nature, and a natural poetic instinct fanned into being by reading accounts of the romantic Minnesingers of old.

Beckmesser, the marker, having pompously ensconced himself in his accustomed curtained recess, with slate and chalk to mark down the faults of the candidate, announced that he was ready to hear the young knight's trial; and Walter immediately burst forth into an enthusiastic song in praise of springtime and maidenhood, so full of true poetry and music that it held the masters spell-bound, in spite of the fact that it completely outraged all their pet rules in every direction.

But the conceited Beckmesser was full of indignation that one so unheedful of the forms and conventions of his own infallible guild should dare to aspire to enter the ranks of the Mastersingers; and before the song was half finished, he burst noisily from behind his curtain, and contemptuously announced that the candidate had already failed many times over, since his slate was scored at least fifty times with faults against the rules, the singer having had no regard at all for the special construction of verse and musical form which he and his friends alone considered to be correct.

The Mastersingers all agreed with the marker's condemnation, with the exception of Hans Sachs, who knew that Beckmesser's verdict was chiefly caused by jealousy; and he himself being the only true poet-musician in the Mastersingers' Guild, alone was able to appreciate Walter's beautiful song, and, seeing that the young knight had a real and lofty genius far beyond anything that his burgher friends could boast of, boldly stood up in his defence, declaring to the outraged company that the stranger's music was of a higher order than their own and consequently not to be judged by their standards, which might not be infallible after all.

But the Mastersingers were not to be convinced, even though their favourite Hans Sachs spoke in favour of the audacious stranger; and so Walter was declared " outsung " and in no way fit to be admitted into the ranks of the Mastersingers.

The young knight, repelled by the Mastersingers' narrow art, from which he had hoped to derive such pleasure, was filled with disappointment and despair; but, finding that he could not hope to gain the hand of his beloved Eva as a Mastersinger, he determined to make an attempt to elope with her that evening.

Eva, being anxious to learn how her lover had fared at his trial, sent her attendant, Magdalena, to get the news from her sweetheart, David, the apprentice of Hans Sachs; and then, upon returning at dusk from a walk with her father, she remained outside the house, to hear what her handmaid had to say. The two girls talked in low tones, for they saw that Hans Sachs (whose shop stood exactly opposite the house of the goldsmith) was still at work; for honest Hans, suspecting the young knight's intention with regard to Eva, had determined to frustrate his plans, in kindness to the imprudent pair, since he loved them both.

Eva was in despair when told by Magdalena of her lover's failure; but, seeing Walter at that moment approaching, she sent her maid within doors, and awaited him with a joy she could not conceal.

The lovers embraced rapturously; and Eva, enthralled by Walter's love for her, readily agreed to his passionate pleading that they should fly together that night. Ere they could make their escape, however, they heard approaching steps; and, hastily concealing themselves behind some bushes, they were forced to wait until the intruder should depart.

The newcomer was none other than Beckmesser, the conceited marker, who, having composed a song to sing at the contest on the morrow, had come now to sing it as a serenade beneath the window of the fair Eva, hoping that the maiden would be thus so favourably impressed by his composition, that she would speak in his favour when he was adjudged the winner, as he so fondly expected to be; and, stationing himself beneath his charmer's chamber window, he commenced his song, which was in reality a very poor one, consisting of inferior poetry and worse melody.

Hans Sachs, hoping now to deter Sir Walter and Eva from their rash act by keeping them in their hiding-place, at once began to sing himself in a very loud voice, to a rollicking tune and merry words; an unexpected performance which was naturally very disconcerting to the serenader.

In a furious rage at this wanton drowning of his sentimental song, with which he had intended to win the heart of Eva, Beckmesser many times shouted to the cobbler to hold his peace; but, finding that Hans refused to listen to his request he resorted to strategy in order to enable his fair mistress to hear his song undisturbed. Approaching the cobbler's shop, he invited Hans to listen to his song, and criticise it, that he might correct any faults there might be in the composition ere performing it on the morrow; and this the cobbler agreed to do, saying that for every fault he detected, he would hammer a nail into the pair of shoes he was at that moment mending for the town clerk, who had been blaming him earlier in the day for being behindhand with his work.

So Beckmesser began his song again, full of delight at observing a maiden's figure appear at the chamber window, imagining this to be his adored one, though it was in reality the waiting-maid, Magdalena, who was

anxiously awaiting the return of her young mistress;
but his rage was soon increased tenfold, for his halt-
ing verses were so full of faulty accents and unmusical discords, that the cobbler's hammer fell with
a thud almost constantly. Ere the song was half
over, Hans ran out of his shop, and, holding up the
finished shoes in triumph, cried mischievously in
imitation of the marker's own manner at the young
knight's examination, " Haven't you done yet? Because I've finished the shoes already, thanks to the
many faults you have made! "

As Beckmesser furiously endeavoured to scream out
the last verses of his song, the apprentice David,
disturbed by this unmusical squalling, opened his
chamber-window; and, seeing his sweetheart, Magdalena, in the chamber opposite, and thinking the
serenade addressed to her, he was seized with jealousy,
and, rushing out into the street, set upon the bold
serenader and began to cudgel him with right good
will.

Taken thus by surprise, Beckmesser began to cry
out for aid, for David was a lusty youth, and was
quickly beating him black and blue; and, aroused by
the sounds of the scuffle, the neighbours came pour-
ing from the houses on every side, and not understanding the reason for the commotion, but stum-
bling in the dark against each other, they began to
quarrel amongst themselves, and a general scrimmage
quickly ensued, in which the mischievous apprentice
friends of David gladly took part, enjoying the riot
as a great joke.

Thinking that in the midst of this scuffle they
might make their escape, Sir Walter tenderly endeavoured to lead Eva round the edge of the crowd;
but Hans Sachs, who had kept his eyes constantly on
the pair, soon frustrated this pretty plan by seizing Walter's arm in his own iron grasp, and at the
same time pushing Eva up the steps of her father's
house, where she was quickly seized and taken within
by Pogner himself, who, having opened his door to

inquire the cause of the scrimmage, was amazed to find his daughter in the midst of the crowd.

Having seen that the half-fainting Eva was safely in her father's care, Hans Sachs, having first caught David and unceremoniously kicked him into his shop, followed himself, dragging the despairing Walter with him; and upon the sound of the night-watchman's horn being heard, the crowd melted away as quickly as it had gathered, so that by the time the sleepy guardian of the peace appeared, the street was deserted and still once more.

Next morning, as Hans, attired in gala dress, ready for the great Festival of St. John's Day, sat in his workshop, the young knight entered from the chamber where he had been resting, and announced to his kind friend that he had just awakened from a beautiful and vivid dream, which he longed to put into song; and the honest, art-loving cobbler entreated him to sing it to him straightway, whilst still fresh in his mind, in the form of a master-song of the correct form, of which he gave him some few hints, declaring that with such a Heaven-sent subject, sung in the richly-flowing stream of melody that was his own priceless gift, he would certainly yet win the maiden he loved so well.

Encouraged thus by the large-hearted Hans, and inspired by his dream, Walter broke forth into a gloriously beautiful song, perfect alike in poetic form and wondrous melody, which the cobbler eagerly wrote down as he sang; and when the song came to an end, Hans, overcome with emotion and joy, hastily pushed the singer back to his chamber, bidding him put on gala raiment, and declaring himself confident of his success in the contest.

Whilst the knight was thus engaged, Beckmesser entered the shop, so stiff from his cudgelling of the night before that he could scarcely walk, and, intending to continue his quarrel with the cobbler; but, seeing the MS. of the song lying on the table, and imagining this to have been composed by Hans, his mood quickly changed, and he asked to be allowed to sing this in the competition, instead of the one he had himself written, since the latter, he added conceitedly, had now without doubt lost the charm it possessed in the ears of his adored mistress, who, having once heard it under such adverse conditions, would probably never care to hear it again.

Hans, knowing well enough that the unmusical town clerk would never be able to enter into the beauty of Walter's love-inspired words, said that he might have the song, bidding him, however, to sing it to a suitable melody; and Beckmesser, more confident than ever of his success, hurried away, full of delight at having thus secured, as he supposed, a song by Hans Sachs, who was acknowledged to be the finest poet amongst the Mastersingers.

A little later in the day, crowds of merry holiday-makers assembled in the large, open meadow on the outskirts of Nuremberg, to hear the great Competition of Song, which had been so eagerly looked forward to by all; and when Eva, the fair prize-maiden, looking more beautiful than ever in her dazzling white robe, and attended by a number of pretty maids-of-honour, had taken her seat upon the daïs which had been set for her, the enthralling business of the day began.

Amidst a sudden hush of expectancy, Hans Sachs rose to announce once again to the people the generous and soul-inspiring prize offered by the art-loving Pogner, to be awarded to the Master Musician whose song should be unanimously declared the most worthy of praise; and when the loud applause which greeted this speech had died away, Beckmesser was called upon to commence his song.

Nervously unrolling the MS. he had all the morning been vainly endeavouring to commit to memory, Beckmesser moved forward, and began his song, singing it to an altogether unsuitable, discordant, and unmusical tune; and in a frantic effort to remember the sense of what he was singing, he mixed up the

words in the most hopeless manner, and, plunging
deeper into the mire of confusion as he proceeded, he
succeeded in completely losing himself, and converted
the poem into an astonishing *pot-pourri* of ludicrous
and meaningless balderdash.

At first, the people listened in amazement, thinking that the infallible marker, usually such a stickler
for the correct rules of Mastersinging, had suddenly
taken leave of his senses; and then, unable to restrain
their merriment any longer, they all burst forth into
a loud peal of derisive laughter, which completely
drowned the ridiculous singer.

In a furious rage of disappointment and wounded
vanity, Beckmesser flung the MS. at the feet of Hans
Sachs, declaring to the people that the cobbler had
schemed thus to disgrace him by foisting his own
bad song upon him; but in spite of his defence, as
he rushed away in a storm of vexation, he was followed by the jeers of the crowd, with whom he was
by no means popular, and who had not desired that
one so pompous and elderly should gain so fair a
prize.

When Beckmesser had disappeared, Hans Sachs
picked up the despised poem, and declared to the
people that the song was a good one, but could only
be properly sung by the person who had composed it,
whose name was not Hans Sachs; and then he called
on Sir Walter von Stolzing, as the composer of the
song, who would, by singing it to them, quickly
prove that he was worthy to be regarded as the very
Mastersinger of Mastersingers.

A hum of admiration swept over the assembled
company as the young knight stepped forward, for
here, indeed, was one whose graceful form, glowing
eyes, and poetry-inspired brow recalled the resplen-
dent Minnesingers of old; and with hearts that
throbbed with excitement, they listened to the rich
joyous flood of melody that now filled the summer
air.

Yes, Hans Sachs was right, and the song was a

noble one, and this was a Heaven-sent singer who laid a magic touch upon their very hearts, and filled them with a rapture almost too intense to be borne; and even the critical Mastersingers who had cavilled at his heedless disregard of their various rules the evening before, were now held spellbound with wonder that song could be so glorious a thing.

As the song came to an end, a deafening burst of applause broke from the assemblage, who, with one accord, declared the young knight to be the winner in the contest; and as the beautiful Eva bent forward to place, with hands that trembled with joy, the wreath of victory upon the brow of the man she loved, a second burst of applause broke forth, for the two were well-matched, and made a fair picture as they stood together.

The Mastersingers now eagerly invited Walter to join their guild as one of themselves, an honour which, however, the young knight proudly refused, since his free spirit could not be curbed within so small a range.

On hearing this, Hans Sachs humorously reproved him for speaking disparagingly of an art which had bestowed so rare a prize upon him; and then he launched forth staunchly into a speech in praise of the honest German art he loved so well, a speech which was received with the wildest enthusiasm by all, for Hans Sachs was the darling of the people of Nuremburg.

Thus the Contest of Song came to an end; and the young knight who had set out so hopefully in search of Art, had found as well a fair bride, whose love should henceforth be the magic golden key that should unlock for him the gates of Fame, Honour, and Glory.

THE NIBELUNGS' RING

(Der Ring der Nibelungen)

PART I

THE RHINEGOLD

(Das Rheingold)

In the rocky depths of the wild Rhine river three lovely water-nymphs—Flosshildr, Woglinda, and Wellgunda—were merrily swimming hither and thither one dusky twilight; for though it was their duty to guard a certain mighty treasure, they found their task a light one, since no one had ever sought to rob them of it.

This evening, however, a visitor came to them at last; and suddenly the Rhine nymphs ceased their gambols in great surprise, on beholding a stranger in their midst. From a deep cleft in the rocks below a hideous black gnome had appeared; for Alberic the Nibelung, being of an adventurous spirit, had wandered upwards from Nibelheim, the underground abode of the gnomes, eager for fresh exploits.

As he now gazed upon the lovely Rhine nymphs, he was suddenly filled with a longing desire to possess one of them as a bride, and uttering a friendly greeting, he endeavoured to ingratiate himself with them. The water-maidens, however, scorned his advances, laughing at his ugly appearance; and when, incited by the fierce desire within him, he vainly tried to seize first one and then another in his grasp, they

61

swam away merrily, leading him on with teasing taunts from rock to rock, until he was quite exhausted.

Presently, on approaching a central rock, upon which the nymphs had ensconced themselves, he was astonished to behold a wondrous gleam of gold issuing from its peak, and delighted at this dazzling radiance, he asked what it was. The maidens replied that the marvellous glow he saw came from the precious treasure they had been set to guard, the Rhinegold, which could only be torn from the rock by one who had forsworn for ever all the delights of love, and who might then shape from it a magic Ring that would gain him mighty power in the world.

On hearing this, Alberic, who had always longed for power, determined to gain the treasure; and loudly declaring that he renounced love and its delights for ever, he climbed the rock, and by a mighty effort wrenched the magic gold from its summit. The Rhine nymphs, now powerless to protect their treasure, dived back into the water with cries of despair, whilst Alberic triumphantly returned to Nibelheim with his prize.

Soon after this incident, the chief of the gods, Wotan, the All-Father, entered into an agreement with two powerful giants, Fasolt and Fafnir, to build him a noble castle in Asgard, the abode of the gods; and in payment for this service, he promised to bestow upon them Freia, the goddess of Youth and Beauty.

Awakening one dawning day upon a flowery mountain-side, where he had been slumbering beside his celestial spouse, Fricka, the goddess of Marriage, he saw the glittering turrets of a glorious mansion upon a distant rocky height, and knew that the task was done; and arousing Fricka, he proudly pointed out to her their new abode, to which he gave the name of Valhalla.

Just then, however, the beautiful Freia fled to them

for protection; and closely pursuing came the two
giants, demanding her as the payment agreed upon
for the task they had just completed.

But Wotan now refused to give up the beloved
Freia, and when the giants, furious at his refusal,
again demanded their rights, he turned eagerly for
help to Loki, the god of Fire and Deceit, at whose
mischievous instigation he had entered into the
compact. Loki had promised the great god to assist
him in preventing the giants from obtaining the
reward agreed upon for their labours, and he now
cunningly related the story of how the Rhine nymphs
had lost their magic gold to Alberic the gnome,
hoping to excite the giants' interest in a treasure
that could secure the holder such mighty power.

His ruse succeeded; for the two giants now declared that they would accept Alberic's treasure in
lieu of the Goddess Freia; and they desired Wotan to
set forth, and rob the gnome at once.

Wotan, however, was furious at being asked to turn
thief, and angrily refused to do their bidding; and
upon this, Fasolt and Fafnir suddenly seized Freia,
and ran off with her, declaring that they would hold
her in pledge until the Rhine Gold treasure was delivered to them.

And now, a dreadful misfortune befell the dwellers
in Asgard; for Freia was the guardian of a magic
apple-tree, the fruit of which, eaten daily, alone
preserved their youth and immortality. Deprived of
the beautiful guardian's care, the apples began to
fade and die, and the gods, consequently, quickly
found themselves growing old and withered, and their
radiant strength departing.

Full of horror, Wotan was now forced to secure
the return of Freia at the price named by the giants;
and, accompanied by Loki, he descended through a
rocky cleft to Nibelheim.

Here they made their way to the cave of Alberic,
whose brother, Mime, they found crouching beside
his blacksmith's forge, smarting from recent blows.

For by this time Alberic had shaped from the Rhine Gold a magic Ring of marvellous power, and by means of it had made himself the ruler of Nibelheim, forcing the unhappy gnomes to slave day and night, amassing treasure-hoards for him. He had also compelled his brother, Mime, the most skilful smith in that land of forges, to make him a *Tarnhelm*, or wishing cap, by means of which he could render himself invisible, or take on the form of any creature he chose.

Having learnt this from Mime, who was even now smarting from the blows of his tyrant-brother, the two gods laid their plans; and when Alberic presently appeared, they greeted him in friendly tones, and invited him to show them the wonderful powers of his *Tarnhelm*.

The gnome, proud of his new treasure, at once put on his wishing-cap, and changed himself into a dragon; and then, at the request of the cunning Loki, he unsuspectingly took on the form of a toad. However, no sooner did the toad appear, than the gods instantly seized it, and binding their captive securely, they triumphantly bore him off to Wotan's mountainside.

Here Alberic, though he had quickly regained his own shape, found himself a prisoner indeed, his precious *Tarnhelm* having been put out of his reach; and the exultant gods refused to set him free until he had agreed to yield up all his mighty treasures. So the wretched dwarf, in order to gain his freedom, was compelled to call upon his gnome-subjects to bring forth the precious hoards they had laid up for him, and to pile them in a heap upon the mountain-side.

When the *Tarnhelm* had been added to the glittering heap of gold and gems, Alberic entreated to be allowed to retain the magic Ring, and upon the request being refused, he passionately laid a curse upon the circlet, declaring that it should bring disaster and death upon every person who should afterwards own it. But in spite of the curse, the Ring was snatched from his finger by Wotan, and then, on being set free, the hapless gnome, robbed of his power, fled back to his own land, vanishing through a cleft in the rock.

A concourse of gods and goddesses had now arrived upon the scene; and presently the giants, Fasolt and Fafnir, also arrived to claim their wages, bringing their hostage with them. At first Wotan also endeavoured to retain the Ring for himself; but the gods refused to yield Freia until they possessed this wonderful talisman as well as the other treasures. Then Erda, the wise goddess of Earth, rose slowly from the ground, and warned the great god that disaster was in store for him the longer he held the now fatal talisman; and at last, overcome by this warning, Wotan tore the Ring from his finger, and flung it upon the treasure-heap.

The giants now took possession of their prize; and upon Freia being set at liberty, all the gods at once regained their pristine youth and strength.

But Alberic's curse had not been a vain one, and no sooner did the giants obtain their treasure than they began to quarrel as to which should have the Ring; and in the fight that quickly ensued, Fasolt was killed. Fafnir, the survivor, then secured the mighty hoard, together with the Ring and *Tarnhelm*, and retired to a certain gloomy cave in a wild, deserted spot; and here, in the form of a huge, fiery dragon, he guarded the prize he had won.

Wotan, over-awed at this immediate proof of the terrible power of Alberic's curse, began to wonder how he could preserve himself and all the gods descended from him; for he, also, had owned the fatal Ring for a time, and, god though he was, his powers were limited. Even when Fricka reminded him that the dazzling abode, Valhalla, was still left to him as a Castle of Refuge, he was little comforted, knowing that it had been obtained at a shameful price that would at length bring about the destruction of the gods, since he, their All-Father, could not escape the

E

curse laid upon him; but he agreed to take possession of the castle.

Since the glittering mansion was separated from them by the great yawning valley of the Rhine, Donner, the god of Thunder, came forward to their aid; and first clearing the cloud-laden, misty air by means of a thunderstorm, he set up a dazzling rainbow-bridge from one mountain top to the other.

It completely spanned the valley; and upon this beautiful arch of radiant light, the gods passed over to take possession of the glorious halls of Valhalla.

PART II

THE VALKYRIE

(*Die Walküre*)

ONE wild and stormy evening, a noble warrior-hero,
named Siegmund, flying weaponless and shieldless
through a dark forest, sought refuge from his pursuing enemies in the first lonely homestead he came
to, and opening the door with eager haste, unceremoniously stepped within.

He found himself in a strange-looking room; for the
house was built around a mighty ash-tree, the huge
trunk of which stood as a pillar in the centre. Finding that the room was empty, Siegmund strode forward to the hearth, and being utterly exhausted by
his late exertions and flight, he stretched himself
upon a bear-skin before the fire, and sank into a
sweet, refreshing slumber.

Soon afterwards, there came forth from an inner
chamber a beautiful but sad-looking maiden—Sieglinde, the mistress of this curious dwelling-place—and
full of surprise at seeing a stranger lying upon the
hearth, she called to him in a low tone.

The sound of the maiden's sweet voice aroused
Siegmund; and raising his head, he asked for a drink.
Sieglinde quickly filled a drinking-horn with water,
and handed it to the warrior, who drank thirstily;
and then, as Siegmund gazed upon the fair beauty
of his benefactress, a thrill of delight passed through
him, and he asked who it was who thus restored
him to life.

Sieglinde, through whose veins an answering thrill had also sped, replied that she was the wife of Hunding, a warrior, in whose house he had found shelter; and to show that he was welcome there, she fetched him a horn of foaming mead, and begged him to drink again. When Siegmund returned the horn, their eyes met in a long, passionate gaze; for love had suddenly entered their hearts, and both felt that their fates would be for ever intertwined.

As they talked together there was a quick step outside, and next moment Hunding, the warrior, entered the room. He was of a fierce, stern, and gloomy countenance; and as his eyes fell upon the stranger standing beside his hearth, a dark scowl swept over his brow. Sieglinde explained in a trembling voice that the stranger had sought shelter in their house, and that she had given him refreshment; and then, extending a somewhat tardy welcome to his guest, Hunding doffed his weapons and bade his wife spread supper for them.

When the three were seated at the table, Hunding curtly demanded his guest's name and history; and Siegmund replied sadly that he was known to the world as "Woful," owing to his misfortunes, and that he and a beloved twin-sister had been born to a famous hero. One evening, when Woful was still but a child, on returning from a forest hunt with his father, a terrible sight had met their eyes; for their home had been burnt and laid waste by enemies, the beautiful mother lay dead, and no trace whatever remained of the tender little maid who had been the sunshine of their lives. Some years later, the warlike hero also suddenly disappeared, and then his unhappy son was left to struggle as best he could with the ill-luck that had followed him all his life. That evening, on passing through the forest, he had rushed to the aid of a poor maiden, whose kinsmen were seeking to wed her to a churl whom she abhorred; but being overwhelmed and disarmed by the fierce tyrants, he had been compelled to flee for his life and take refuge in the first homestead he came to.

On hearing this last part of the story, Hunding's brow grew dark; and he declared with suppressed anger that they were his kinsfolk whom Woful had attacked, adding that he himself had been called to their aid, but arriving too late to be of assistance, had returned to his house, only to find the flying foe upon his own hearth.

Siegmund, seeing that he had thus unwittingly sought shelter in the abode of an enemy, felt that his last hour had come, since he had no weapons for his defence; but Hunding, being bound by the laws of hospitality not to harm his guest till the morrow, declared that he was safe for that night, but should die with morning light.

He then bade his wife prepare his evening draught, and retire for the night; but as Sieglinde moved towards the inner chamber, she threw a tender, sympathising glance upon the despondent Siegmund. Then Hunding, having seen that the door was fastened, took up his weapons with a triumphant look at his doomed guest, and also departed to the sleeping-chamber; and Siegmund, left alone, sank upon the hearth with troubled thoughts.

Presently, as he lay gazing into the dying embers of the fire, the door of the inner chamber was softly opened, and the beautiful Sieglinde came towards him in haste, declaring that he might now depart in safety, since Hunding lay wrapped in helpless slumber, she having mixed a narcotic with his evening draught. She added that a wonderful weapon also lay ready to his hand; and then, returning the tender glance bestowed upon her by Siegmund, she began to tell him a strange story.

On the day she was wedded to Hunding against her will, having been forced to the deed by fierce ravishers who had stolen her from her home in early childhood, a stranger, wrapped in a dark cloak, had suddenly entered this very hall, and plunging a shining sword deep down to the hilt in the ash-tree's stem, had declared that it possessed magic qualities, and should become the prize of whichever hero could pluck it forth. All the warriors at the festive board had tried to wrench the sword from its sheath, but in vain; and Sieglinde added that she knew by the kindly glance bestowed upon her by the stranger, whose features had reminded her of the father she had been stolen from, that the magic weapon was reserved for some brave hero who should one day come to offer her his love and help, and who, her heart whispered, now stood before her.

These words filled Siegmund with an intoxication of joy; and no longer able to quell the love that already surged in his heart, he clasped the beautiful maiden in his arms with rapture. But as Sieglinde gazed upon her beloved, his features and glances suddenly reminded her of the stranger who had plunged the sword in the tree; and on learning from Siegmund that his father had been known as Volsung, she exclaimed that that was the name of her own father, whose features had been reflected in those of the stranger who had appeared on her wedding morn.

Siegmund, quickly realising that it was his long-lost twin-sister who stood before him, and whose love he had won, embraced her with even greater joy than before; and knowing now that his mysterious father, Volsung, had placed the sword in the ash-tree to be plucked thence by his own son only, he hastened to the mighty tree and triumphantly drew the weapon forth, announcing its name to be " Needful." Then the enraptured lovers, hand locked in hand, rushed forth joyously into the sweet spring night; and hastening with glad footsteps through the moon-lit forest, they sought a place of refuge from the vengeance of Hunding, who, they knew, would follow them on awakening from the effects of the narcotic.

Now Siegmund and Sieglinde, though they knew it not, were in reality the twin-children of the great god Wotan, who, in the guise of the hero Volsung, had wooed and won a beautiful maiden of the earth; and from the first naught but misery had fallen to the lot of the ill-fated pair.

As soon as Wotan's celestial wife, Fricka, the goddess of Marriage and upholder of conjugal bonds, knew of the unholy love of Siegmund and Sieglinde, and of their flight from Hunding, she was filled with indignation; and summoning her roving and inconstant husband, she poured forth angry reproaches upon him for countenancing this violation of her laws. She demanded that the recreant lovers should be overtaken and punished, and that Siegmund's magic sword should be broken; and knowing that Wotan had already despatched one of his attendant war-maidens, the beautiful Valkyrie, Brynhildr, to assist his son against the pursuing Hunding, she bade him instantly recall her.

It was in vain that Wotan, who really loved his earth-born children, pleaded for the unhappy lovers; and the angry goddess gave him no peace until he promised to cause Siegmund to be vanquished by his avenger.

So the great god reluctantly called back the Valkyrie, Brynhildr; and when the beautiful war-maiden appeared before him, clad in dazzling mail, fully armed and mounted on a fiery celestial steed, he sadly commanded her to give assistance to the wronged Hunding, instead of to Siegmund, as he had at first bade her. Brynhildr, who knew that Wotan still longed to help his son, went forth upon her mission with a heavy heart, and soon came up with the fleeing lovers.

After wandering onwards for many days, only stopping for necessary rest, Siegmund and his stolen bride had at length come to a wild, rocky height; but even here they did not feel safe, for they knew that Hunding was quickly following on their track. But Sieglinde was so much exhausted by her long journey that she could go no farther; and sinking upon a sheltering ledge, she presently fell into a troubled sleep.

As Siegmund watched beside the sleeping form of his beloved one, he suddenly beheld the dazzling figure of the beautiful war-maiden, Brynhildr; and knowing that the Valkyries only appeared to heroes doomed to fall in battle, he asked in trembling tones whom she sought. Brynhildr answered solemnly that she had come to bear him, Siegmund the Volsung, hence with her to Valhalla, at the command of Wotan; but when Siegmund eagerly asked if Sieglinde would accompany him there, she replied that the maiden must remain on earth.

Then Siegmund passionately declared that he would forego all the celestial glories of Valhalla if he might not share them with his beloved one; adding that with his magic sword, Needful, he would gain the victory in the approaching fight, and thus defeat Wotan of his prey.

Now when Brynhildr saw what a passionate love it was that bound these two young hearts, she was filled with tender pity; and at last, after a short struggle with herself, she resolved to disobey the command of Wotan, and give her assistance to the lovers, instead of to their enemy.

Presently the young warrior heard the sound of horn-calls coming nearer and nearer; and soon afterwards Hunding came in sight. A violent thunderstorm now began to rage, and the sombre gloom of the wild scene was constantly illumined by the awful glare of lightning; but, heedless of the warring elements, Siegmund dashed forward to meet the vengeful Hunding as he appeared on the craggy height, and quickly clashed swords with him.

The noise of the storm awakened Sieglinde; and she uttered a shriek of terror as a brilliant flash of lightning revealed to her the furiously fighting forms of Hunding and Siegmund, with the Valkyrie, Brynhildr, soaring defensively over the latter, guarding him with her shield. But at this moment there was an unexpected interruption; for Wotan himself, enraged by the Valkyrie's disobedience to his will, and bound by his oath to his celestial spouse, suddenly swooped down upon the combatants, with anger in his mien.

Terrified at this awful apparition of the all-powerful god, Brynhildr retreated before him; and as she did so, Siegmund's magic sword broke upon the outstretched mighty spear of Wotan, leaving him thus the prey of the triumphant Hunding, who quickly buried his weapon in the defenceless breast of his enemy.

As her vanquished lover uttered his last dying gasp, Sieglinde sank senseless to the ground; but Brynhildr snatched her up instantly, and mounting her fiery steed that stood waiting near, she rode wildly away with her prize.

For a few moments Wotan gazed down sorrowfully upon the prostrate form of the hero-son he would so gladly have saved; and then, in a terrible outburst of wrath and grief, he killed the conquering Hunding, and disappeared on the wings of the storm in pursuit of the flying Brynhildr.

The beautiful war-maiden rode at desperate speed; but, after travelling an immense distance, her noble steed at last fell exhausted at the top of a high rocky mountain. Upon the summit of this mountain, a band of mounted Valkyries in full armour had gathered to rest on their way to Valhalla, each with the dead body of a fallen warrior lying across her saddle-bag; and to these war-maidens, her sisters, Brynhildr hastened to beg assistance, bearing Sieglinde with her.

She quickly told them her story, and begged for a horse to continue her flight; but when the Valkyries knew that she was flying from the wrath of their beloved All-Father, they refused to give her aid, fearing lest Wotan's anger should fall upon them also, if they protected one who had disobeyed him.

Seeing that she could thus no longer protect the

now conscious Sieglinde, Brynhildr bade her fly on-
ward alone, towards a certain forest ever shunned by
Wotan; and when the poor maiden declared that
she no longer desired to live, the inspired Valkyrie
earnestly besought her not to despair, since she should
become the mother of the greatest hero of the world,
who should be called Siegfried. At the same time,
she placed in her hands the broken pieces of Siegmund's magic sword, which she had seized as he
fell to the ground; and she desired Sieglinde to keep
the fragments for her son, who should forge them
once more into a weapon of wondrous power.

Comforted, and filled with joy on hearing this
prophecy, Sieglinde, no longer despairing, was eager
to save herself from harm; and bestowing a grateful
blessing upon her self-sacrificing protector, she
quickly rushed away towards the gloomy forest
indicated.

Amidst appalling thunder and lightning Wotan
now appeared upon the mountain top; and as Brynhildr stood humbly before him, with downcast mien,
the angry god declared that for her disobedience to
him, she should be a Valkyrie no longer, and that,
deprived of divinity and the sweet joys of Valhalla,
she should be doomed to lie in an enchanted sleep,
for the first passing churl to awaken and call his own.

On hearing her terrible sentence, Brynhildr sank
upon her knees; and with a despairing cry, she implored the All-Father not to leave her to become the
prey of any mere braggart, but to place a circle of
fire around the rock upon which she must lie in
charmed sleep, that she might at least not be awakened by any but a hero valiant enough to brave the
flames to gain her.

For some time Wotan refused to grant her plea;
but at last he yielded, overcome by the tenderness he
still felt for her, for Brynhildr had ever been the
best beloved of all his war-maidens. He declared that
he would call forth such fiery flames to protect her
slumbers as should scare away all timid cravens, and

that only one who had never known fear should awaken her—the greatest hero of the world; and Brynhildr was filled with joy and gratitude, knowing that this mighty feat was reserved for the yet unborn hero-son of Siegmund and Sieglinde.

Wotan now gently kissed the beautiful Valkyrie upon both eyes, which instantly closed in slumber; and bearing her tenderly in his arms, he laid her upon a low, moss-covered rock covering her graceful mail-clad form with the long shield she had borne so bravely. Then, striking the rock three times with his spear, he uttered an invocation to the god Loki to come to his aid, and out leapt a stream of fiery flames, which quickly surrounded the mountain top; and with a last long look of affection at the sleeping maiden, the god returned to his celestial abode.

But the fair Brynhildr lay wrapped in peaceful slumber upon her fire-encircled couch; and though many bold travellers longed to possess the lovely maiden, none were found willing to brave the scorching flames—a deed that awaited the coming of the world's greatest hero, Siegfried the Fearless.

PART III

SIEGFRIED

Mime the Nibelung stood working at his forge one summer day in the gloomy forest cavern that served him as a dwelling-place; and as he hammered at a fine long sword he had laid upon the anvil, he was filled with despondency, knowing that, in spite of all his skill in forging, he could not make a sword that would not be splintered at the first mighty stroke of the noble youth for whom it was intended.

For Mime, though but a hideous gnome of evil disposition, and full of guile, had been the means of preserving the precious infant life of Siegfried, the promised hero-son of Siegmund and Sieglinde; and he had nourished him with great care, knowing that this child was destined, in years to come, to slay Fafnir, the giant dragon that guarded the mighty treasure of his Nibelung brother, Alberic.

He cunningly hoped by means of Siegfried to obtain this coveted treasure for himself; and so he kept the child ignorant of the secret of the Rhinegold, and of his own high birth. As Siegfried grew to manhood, he had no knowledge of his true parentage, though he utterly refused to regard Mime as his father; for in spite of his protecting care, he hated the dwarf, feeling unconsciously that he had only preserved him for his own evil ends.

Mime knew this, and feared him accordingly; and as he now stood working at his forge this summer day, he trembled as he thought of the youth's wonder-

76

ful strength, for every sword he had yet made for him, Siegfried had only contemptuously snapped in half.

Just as he finished the sword, Siegfried himself dashed boisterously into the cave, leading by a leash a great bear he had caught in the forest; for fear was unknown to the hero-son of Sieglinde, and savage beasts he but regarded as his play-fellows.

He was a noble-looking youth of dazzling beauty, mighty strength, and dauntless courage as befitted a descendant of the great god, Wotan; and his contempt for the puny Mime was quickly shown by the careless manner in which, in mere wanton mischief, he drove the fierce bear round the cave after the wretched gnome, who shrank back in abject fear.

At last, having laughingly driven the growling beast back to the forest, Siegfried returned, and demanded the new sword he had bidden Mime forge for him; and the dwarf timidly handed him the blade he had just finished, which would have been regarded as a mighty weapon by any ordinary mortal.

But Siegfried laughed derisively as he took up the sword to test its strength; and striking it but once upon the anvil, the steel immediately shivered to pieces.

To stem the torrent of wrath that now burst upon him, Mime whiningly implored Siegfried to remember the loving care he had ever shown for him since infancy; but the youth declared that he hated the sight of the gnome, and despised the pretended love he professed for him, since he knew him to be at heart false and evil.

He then demanded to be told who were his parents, and how he came to be left in the charge of a puny dwarf; and Mime, terrified at the authoritative flash in the eyes of Siegfried, and not daring to deceive him longer, told him in trembling tones all that he knew. He said that he had found in the forest one day a beautiful woman, named Sieglinde, who lay in tears and deep suffering; and carrying her to his cave, he had tended her with care. She gave birth to a child during the night, and dying almost immediately afterwards, had left the babe to the care of Mime, bidding him call her son by the name of Siegfried.

Filled with emotion as he listened to this sad story, Siegfried next demanded some proof of its truth; and very reluctantly Mime presently produced the pieces of a broken sword, which he said the dying woman had also left in his charge for her son, whose hero-father, she declared, had used it in his last fight. Overjoyed at the possession of this great treasure, which proved that his father had been a noble warrior, Siegfried now commanded Mime to forge the pieces afresh into a mighty sword once more, and enthusiastically declaring that with his father's weapon he would win himself renown, he rushed forth into the forest to tell his joy to the birds and beasts he loved so well.

But Mime was left in despair; for though he had many times in secret tried to weld the broken pieces of the magic sword, Needful, he had never yet succeeded, and knew it was beyond his skill to do so.

As the dwarf stood despondently at his anvil, a stranger, wrapped in a dark mantle, suddenly entered the cave and sat down to rest by the hearth; and though he called himself a Wanderer, Mime soon learnt to his terror, from the stranger's huge spear causing thunder to mutter as it struck the ground, that it was in reality the great god Wotan who had thus invaded his dwelling.

Although ill-received by the dwarf, the Wanderer calmly kept his seat; and in the course of conversation, he announced that Mime should fall a prey to the just wrath of one who had never known fear, and who alone possessed the power to forge the mighty sword, Needful.

With these ominous words the stranger vanished, and as Mime shrank back to his forge, trembling, Siegfried returned from the forest, and demanded his sword. The dwarf declared that he had not skill enough to forge the broken blade, and he added that it could only be restored by one who had never felt fear.

Upon Siegfried eagerly demanding what this fear was, Mime tried to describe the feeling to him; and the youth declared that he had no knowledge of such tremblings, but was curious to experience them. Then Mime craftily remarked that he knew of a terrible giant dragon, named Fafnir, who would quickly teach him what fearing was; and Siegfreid exclaimed impetuously that the dwarf should conduct him to this monster without delay.

He then took up the fragments of the magic sword, declaring that he alone, who knew not fear, would restore the weapon; and filing down the steel, he melted it in a crucible, and began to forge it afresh. Amidst the roaring of the bellows and the clang of the falling hammer, Mime sat lost in meditation, wondering how he could turn the youth's power to his own purposes; and at last an evil idea flashed across his brain.

He would let the hero slay the dragon and even secure the treasure; and then, when exhausted by his exertions, he would offer him a cooling draught containing a deadly poison, which should instantly cause his death, and the great prize would thus fall into the hands of Mime the Nibelung.

Siegfried had now fashioned his sword, and was singing gleefully as he hammered it on the anvil, calling it lovingly by name, and finishing it off with wondrous skill; and by the time the gnome had brewed his fatal draught, the magic blade, Needful, was completely restored.

With a loud shout of joy Siegfried seized the mighty weapon, and struck it with all his force upon the anvil to test its strength; and the blow was so great that the anvil split from top to bottom, and fell asunder with a terrific crash.

But Needful remained bright and unscratched; and

swinging the wonderful sword exultingly over his head Siegfried rushed out of the cave, calling on the awed and shrinking Mime to lead him to the dragon's den. The dwarf, quickly recovering himself, and remembering the prize in store for him, took up the horn containing the fatal draught he had brewed; and joining Siegfried immediately, he led him unerringly through the forest to the wild spot where Fafnir's cave was situated.

Here Alberic the Nibelung had been awaiting the dragon's death for many years; and having learnt this very day from Wotan, the Wanderer, of the near approach of Siegfried, he had slipped back into a rocky cleft to watch what happened.

Soon afterwards, Siegfried and Mime came forth from the forest; but the timid dwarf did not dare to remain long near the cave, and quickly departed to hide, after telling the youth that the dragon would soon appear. The young hero presently blew a long, loud blast upon his hunting-horn; and almost immediately afterwards, the terrible giant dragon, Fafnir, came out from his cave, demanding who summoned him.

Siegfried stared at the great beast in amazement; but not a single spark of alarm was in his brave heart as he boldly announced that he had come to learn what fearing was. Fafnir replied that he was overbold, since he should now serve him as food; but upon this, Siegfried, having no mind to provide a meal for the unwieldy creature, though fearless still, drew his sword, Needful, and smilingly sprang forward to meet his enemy.

With fire and poisonous fumes issuing from his nostrils, the dragon rushed upon him; but as it raised its huge body, Siegfried dashed boldly beneath the gaping jaws, and buried his sword in the monster's breast.

As the dragon rolled over, dead, Siegfried drew his sword triumphantly from its body; but in so doing, he accidentally tasted the creature's blood.

Suddenly he discovered, to his joy, that he could now understand the language of the birds around him; and being especially attracted by the notes of a pretty wood-bird, he went nearer to listen to what it had to say. The wood-bird told him to enter the cave, and possess himself of the dragon's treasure, adding that if only he gained the *Tarnhelm* and magic Ring, he could make himself lord of the whole world.

Full of joy, Siegfried rushed into the cave; and at that moment Mime and Alberic came forth from opposite directions, scowling with surprise and anger as they recognised each other. They instantly began to quarrel as to which should have the treasure; but when Siegfried presently issued from the cave, with the Ring on his finger and the wishing-cap tucked into his belt, Alberic departed, content to let his curse take effect upon the spoiler.

As Siegfried passed under the trees, the wood-bird again spoke to him: and this time his feathered friend warned him that Mime was his enemy, and meant to poison him in order to obtain the treasures he had won. The youth, having always suspected the dwarf of evil intentions, was thus put upon his guard; and when Mime presently drew near with insinuating smile, and pleasantly offered him the horn of poison as a " cooling drink," he instantly plunged his sword into the traitor's heart.

As the crafty dwarf fell dead at his feet, the wood-bird spoke yet once again; and in sweet, thrilling tones, it now told him of a glorious bride whom he might win—the beautiful fallen Valkyrie, Brynhildr, who still slept upon her rocky fastness, surrounded by fire, and waiting for the one fearless hero of the world to brave the flames and possess her.

Filled with rapture at the thought that the joys of love might thus be his, Siegfried eagerly desired to know in which direction so fair a prize lay; and for answer, the pretty wood-bird spread its wings and fluttered along in front to show him the way. Through miles and miles of forest depths the

F

feathered guide flew without resting; and then, when night had passed and the rosy dawn appeared, it suddenly vanished, and Siegfried, finding himself at the foot of a wild mountain, the rocky top of which was encircled by fire, knew that he had arrived at his goal.

But as he approached the mountain-side his path was suddenly blocked by a stranger. This was none other than Wotan, the Wanderer, who still roamed the world, conscious of his approaching doom, which should be brought nearer by this same radiant Volsung youth, and who, having vainly sought advice from the wise goddess Erda, now half-heartedly hoped to oppose the hero himself.

Seeing a stranger barring his path with extended spear, Siegfried drew his magic blade, Needful, and with a mighty stroke hewed the spear in two pieces, upon which a blinding flash of lightning rent the air, followed by a loud crash of thunder. Knowing now that it was useless to withstand this hero-youth who had thus destroyed his weapon of power, Wotan vanished in a cloud of darkness, and retreating in despair to Valhalla, he there awaited the Twilight of the Gods, which he knew was now quickly approaching, since he, the mightiest of them all, had been defeated.

But Siegfried, free to pursue his way once more, dashed joyfully up the mountain-side, and plunging fearlessly through the fierce encircling flames, he reached the rock beyond in safety. Here the Valkyrie, Brynhildr, still lay peacefully slumbering; and gently removing her protecting shield and helmet, Siegfried, entranced, stood gazing in breathless silence upon her dazzling loveliness. A passionate love surged up in his quickly-beating heart; and kneeling beside the fair maiden, he pressed a tender kiss upon her lips.

Instantly Brynhildr opened her beautiful eyes, and rising from her rocky couch greeted Siegfried with joy, telling him that she had loved him all through her charmed sleep, knowing that he alone should awaken her to life once more.

Then Siegfried, enraptured, clasped her in his arms, entreating her to accept his love; and though Brynhildr at first shrank back, offended at the touch of a mortal, she could not long fight against the answering passion awakened in her own breast. Remembering that her divinity was now lost for ever, she placed her hand in Siegfried's with joy; and as the hero held his beautiful bride in his arms, he felt that the dark night-time of his early years had at last dawned into a glorious day-time of light and joy.

PART IV

THE TWILIGHT OF THE GODS

(Die Götterdämmerung)

WHEN night-time fell, after the meeting of Brynhildr and Siegfried, the three Nornir, or Fates, appeared on the Valkyrie's fire-encircled rock, and crouching amidst the rugged stones, began to sing as they spun their golden cord of the runes of Destiny.

But although the radiant lovers slumbered sweetly in a neighbouring cave, and all the world around seemed calm and peaceful, the weird song of the three dread Sisters was full of gloom and sadness; for they knew that, owing to the fatal power of the Nibelung's curse, disaster was about to fall, not only upon these lovers, but also upon the dwellers in Asgard, whose doom was quickly approaching.

Suddenly, as they sang, their rope of Destiny broke asunder; and with wild, despairing cries the three Nornir disappeared, knowing now that the Twilight of the Gods would soon begin.

The night wore on, and when daylight appeared the lovers issued from the cave: Siegfried, in full armour, with his mighty sword girdled about him, and Brynhildr leading her horse by its bridle. For the beautiful Valkyrie would not keep her hero, dearly though she loved him, from gaining glory and honour in the world; and Siegfried, having already learned much of her divine wisdom, was now about to set forth in search of fresh exploits and adventures.

84

For a parting gift to his love, Siegfried placed his magic Ring upon Brynhildr's finger as the sign of their troth, as yet knowing naught of its fatal power; and Brynhildr, in return, bestowed upon him her noble horse, Grani. The lovers swore to be true to each other, and then, after a passionate farewell, they parted.

After many wanderings, Siegfried, following the course of the Rhine, came to the Hall of the Gibichungs, or Burgundian tribe. Here a powerful king, named Gunther, reigned, and with him lived his beautiful sister, Gudrun, and their half-brother, Hagen, whose father was none other than the wretched gnome, Alberic.

Now, Hagen, though so keen-witted as to be the chosen adviser of his royal half-brother, had also inherited the evil qualities and greed of his gnome-father; and hearing of the approach of the hero, Siegfried, whose wonderful exploits were by this time world-renowned, he laid a cunning plan, by means of which the Gibichungs might win, or at least share, the fearless one's power and wealth.

Relating the story of the fire-encircled Valkyrie, he pointed out to Gunther that Brynhildr would make him a radiant bride, and that if Gudrun could be wedded to Siegfried, they would thus secure the Nibelung's treasure, which would gain them the mastery of the whole world. He suggested that in order to carry out this plan they should give Siegfried, on his arrival, a magic draught they possessed, by means of which he should forget his love for Byrnhildr, and conceive a passion for Gudrun; and Gunther and his sister, being dazzled at the prospect of being so nobly mated, gladly agreed to the scheme, whilst Hagen, cunningly keeping back his knowledge of Brynhildr's and Siegfried's vows of love, rejoiced, because of the opportunity that would occur for securing the treasure he coveted.

So when Siegfried arrived in the Gibichungs' land he was met on the banks of the Rhine by Hagen, and conducted at once to the royal Hall; and here he received a joyous welcome from King Gunther and his fair sister.

Siegfried was greatly pleased with his kindly welcome; and when Gudrun presently offered him a well-filled drinking-horn, in token of friendship and hospitality, he gladly drank off its contents to the health of his beloved Brynhildr.

But the magic love-potion had been mingled with the draught, and no sooner had he set down the horn than the likeness of Brynhildr faded from his mind, and all memory of his love for her became a blank. It seemed to him that the fair Gudrun was the first maiden he had ever beheld, and a passionate desire to possess her suddenly grew up within him.

Gudrun beheld his ardent glances with great joy, for an answering love had quickly sprung up in her own heart for the noble hero before her. Taking her willing hand in his, Siegfried led the maiden, who now possessed his whole heart, to her royal brother, and eagerly requested her hand in marriage; and to this Gunther gave his consent on condition that the Valkyrie, Brynhildr, was secured as a bride for himself. Siegfried gladly agreed to go through the fire once more, and woo Brynhildr for his new friend; and when the two had sworn an oath of brotherhood, they set out together to begin their enterprise at once.

In a royal barque they sailed down the Rhine a certain distance, and then when the Valkyrie's rock came in sight, Siegfried bade Gunther remain in the boat, whilst he himself went forward alone to climb the mountain. By means of his *Tarnhelm*, or wishing-cap, he took on the form and appearance of Gunther—the two having agreed that the martial maiden must be wooed and won by Siegfried in the likeness of the king—and promising to be loyal and faithful to his oath, the young hero began to climb the rocky height.

Brynhildr had just received a visit from her

Valkyrie sister, Valtrauta, who had come to entreat
her to restore the Nibelung's fatal Ring to the Rhine
nymphs once more, as the only remaining hope of
saving the dwellers in Asgard; for Wotan had now
gathered the gods together in Valhalla—around which
he had caused to be piled a forest of faggots from
the world's ash-tree, hewn down at his command—
and all were silently and sadly awaiting their approaching doom, the dreaded Twilight, that meant
for them destruction. The only glimpse of hope now
left was for the mighty Ring to be returned to the
Rhine, when its curse upon men and gods would
become void; and on learning this from the beloved
All-Father, Valtrauta had mounted her war-horse and
flown at once to her fallen sister, who she knew
possessed the Ring.

But Brynhildr, cut off as she was from the joys of
Valhalla, would not part with her love-token, which
was more precious to her than all the dwellers in
Asgard; and in spite of the passionate entreaties of
Valtrauta, she utterly refused to give up the Ring.

Finding that her pleading was in vain, the despairing Valkyrie was compelled to depart; and no sooner
had she gone, than Siegfried, in the form and garb
of Gunther, sprang fearlessly through the zone of
fire, and advancing towards Brynhildr, whom he
regarded as a stranger, announced calmly, in a disguised voice, that having braved the flames he had
come to possess her as a bride.

Full of horror at being thus wooed by a stranger
during the absence of her hero-lover, Brynhildr
shrank back, and indignantly refused to yield herself
to this bold intruder, receiving strength from her
magic Ring; but upon her talisman being wrested
from her by the superior force of Siegfried, she
became powerless, and was compelled to submit to
his will. Siegfried now led her to the cave as their
bridal chamber, but, mindful of his oath and loyalty
to Gunther, whose wooing he had so strangely undertaken, he laid his sword, Needful, between them.

Next day, at dawn, the disguised Siegfried took the bride he had won for another by the hand, and led her safely through the flames and down the mountain-side, and on being met at the river-side by Gunther, he instantly vanished by means of his *Tarnhelm*, and transported himself to the Gibichungs' Hall. So when the true Gunther took her by the hand, Brynhildr regarded him as her wooer of the night before, and the pair entered the barque.

Now, during the absence of Gunther and Siegfried, Hagen had been visited in a vision by his gnome-father, Alberic, who besought him to seek quickly an opportunity to kill Siegfried, and so secure from him the magic Ring by means of which the Nibelung might regain his lost power; and Hagen gladly agreed to use his craft for this purpose.

When Gunther returned with Brynhildr to the Gibichungs' Hall, great preparations were made to celebrate the two marriages in splendid state, and all the vassals and warriors quickly assembled to join in the revels.

All this time Brynhildr had remained submissive and downcast; but now, on entering the Hall with Gunther and finding herself confronted by Siegfried, who led Gudrun by the hand, she started violently and gazed on him with utter astonishment. Suddenly observing the magic Ring upon his finger, the true identity of the bold wooer who had intruded upon her rocky fastness flashed across her mind, and, full of furious anger at the discovery, she announced to all the company that she had been betrayed, and that Siegfried, in his wooing of her in disguise, had dishonoured their King.

Siegfried fearlessly defended himself, declaring that he had been loyal to his trust; but his explanations were designedly confounded by Hagen, who, for his own evil purposes, used his cunning wit to persuade all that the great hero had indeed acted as a base traitor.

Siegfried, however, having a clear conscience, still

declared his innocence; and taking the hand of Gudrun, whom he now loved passionately owing to the effect of the love-potion, he led her gaily to join in the revels, followed by most of the company.

But Brynhildr and Gunther remained in their places, overcome with indignation, still believing Siegfried to be false; and seeing them alone, Hagen joined them, and with cunning words strengthened their suspicions and persuaded them that it was their duty to avenge themselves for the ill that had been done them. He at last obtained their consent to the murder of Siegfried, which he agreed to carry out himself at a hunting party next day; and having arranged this, they rejoined the revellers, and the wedding rejoicings went forward once more.

Next day, a grand royal hunt was organised, and Siegfried, in eager pursuit of prey, found himself at one time alone on the bank of the river. As he stood there a moment, gazing into the water, the three lovely Rhine maidens, Flosshildr, Woglinda, and Wellgunda, swam towards the shore and gave him glad greeting, knowing that this was the great hero who now possessed their long-lost treasure; and in coaxing tones they entreated him to restore the magic Ring to them.

Siegfried, however, refused to listen to their pleadings, even when the nymphs told him that if he retained it longer, the talisman would quickly bring death upon him; and as the Rhine maidens swam away disconsolately, he laughed aloud at their warning.

At that moment, Gunther, Hagen, and the rest of the hunting party joined him, and sitting down to rest upon the river bank, the huntsmen began to feast and make merry together. To amuse his new friends, Siegfried began to tell them the story of his life and adventures; but just as he was relating how he had scaled the fire-encircled mountain, Hagen crept softly forward and suddenly stabbed him in the back with his hunting-spear, announcing to the dismayed onlookers that the deed was done in retribution for the hero's betrayal of their King.

Siegfried sank to the ground immediately; and the effect of the magic potion of forgetfulness waning as his life-blood welled forth, all his old love for the beautiful Valkyrie he had so innocently betrayed returned to bless his last moments, and with Brynhildr's name upon his lips, he died.

The dead hero's body was quickly borne back to the royal Hall; and when the fair Gudrun beheld the lifeless form of her husband of a day, she fell senseless to the ground, overcome by despair.

Hagen and Gunther now began to quarrel as to which should possess the magic Ring; and in the furious fight that ensued Gunther was killed.

Loud cries of woe quickly arose, and in the dismay and confusion that followed, Brynhildr hastened forward. At sight of the dead Siegfried, she was filled with utmost grief, and learning from the reviving and sorrowing Gudrun of his innocence, and remembering naught but her passionate love for him, she firmly resolved to perish with her hero.

In a commanding tone none dared to disobey she silenced the noise and confusion around her, and bade the warriors instantly to build up a funeral pyre upon the banks of the Rhine; and when this had been done, the dead body of Siegfried was laid upon it. She then tenderly placed his magic Ring upon her finger, and seizing a lighted torch, set the faggots ablaze.

She now understood that through her alone the sin of the great All-Father must be atoned for, and that by her sacrifice of Love, the world should be redeemed. The curse of the Ring would also be removed by her death, for with her ashes the fatal Gold would be restored to the Rhine.

Thus nobly resolving to sacrifice herself, she desired two Ravens hovering near—the messengers of Wotan —to return to the great god so sadly awaiting his end, and announce to him that his destiny was about to be fulfilled; and also to bid the god Loki, who still guarded the rock upon which she had lain in a charmed sleep, to depart with his fire to Valhalla.

She then mounted her faithful steed, Grani, and as the flames sprang brightly upwards, leaped high with him into the midst of the burning pyre, and perished beside the corpse of her hero-lover. As the flames died away, the river suddenly rose, and overflowing its banks, covered the remains of the funeral pile; and at the same moment, the three Rhine nymphs swam up to secure their Gold.

Hagen made a last frantic effort to reach the talisman by plunging into the flood; but being seized by the nymphs, he was dragged beneath the waves and drowned.

So the Rhine maidens at last regained their precious treasure, and the curse of the Ring was removed; but the dwellers in Asgard were doomed, for Loki had already accomplished his mission.

Suddenly a fiery, crimson glow appeared in the heavens, ever spreading and increasing to a dazzling brilliancy; and as the warriors and mourners gazed with awe upon this wondrous sight, they saw that Valhalla, with all its glorious array of gods and heroes, was already engulfed in an ocean of leaping flames.

The Twilight of the Gods had come!

PARSIFAL

IN the early days of Christianity, when troublous times beset the path of the true believer, the Holy Grail, or Sacred Cup from which our Saviour had drank at the Last Supper, and which had afterwards received the blood that flowed from His pierced side as He lay upon the Cross, had been brought, together with the spear which had wounded Him, by a company of angels into the mountainous district of Northern Spain; and here the holy relics were reverently received with joy and gratitude by the good King, Titurel, who built for them a Temple-Sanctuary and castle upon the beautiful mountain of Monsalvat, where they were constantly guarded by brave knights of stainless purity and integrity.

Great was the reward of their faithful service, for the Holy Grail possessed miraculous powers, bestowing both bodily as well as spiritual strength and nourishment upon its guardians, giving them such means of grace that they were able to perform mighty deeds for the good of mankind; and with the Sacred Spear, the righteous King Titurel was able to keep at bay the infidels and all who were opposed to Christianity, and who struggled vainly to break down his stronghold.

None but the pure and innocent could approach the holy sanctuary, or hope to derive benefit from its wondrous powers; for the Grail Knights, by reason of their own spotless purity, could read the hearts of all comers, and sternly repulsed any who were unworthy.

Thus it came about that when Klingsor, the most

wicked of all magicians, and the ruler of the heathen
and infidel races, once sought the Grail, hoping to
be released from his many sins, partly seized by a
temporary fit of remorse, but chiefly for the means
of worldly advancement and power, he was denied
entrance to the sacred temple; for the Guardian of
the Grail saw clearly into the deceitful heart of the
sorcerer, and reading there, as in a book, his impious
and unholy thoughts, he drove him back with
horror.

Rendered furious by his ignominious defeat,
Klingsor determined to be revenged, and for this purpose he set up an Enchanted Castle on the southern
slopes of the same mountain, surrounding it with
luxuriant gardens in which he placed sirens of dazzling beauty, who with their seductive charms should
ensnare the Knights of the Grail who wandered that
way, and lure them by unholy passions and evil spells
to destruction from which there should be no return.

Many were the knights thus enticed from the paths
of purity to a life of sinful pleasures and soul-destroy-
ing voluptuousness.

Thus many years passed away; and, at last, good
King Titurel, now well-stricken in years, felt himself
growing too old to perform the sacred offices of the
Holy Grail any longer; so he invested his son,
Amfortas, the handsomest and most glorious of all
the knights, with the royal mantle and made him
King in his stead.

The young King Amfortas, impatient of Klingsor's
evil influence, determined to vanquish the wicked
Enchanter and put an end to his dangerous magic;
and, armed with the sacred spear, he went fearlessly
forth one day upon his great mission. But Klingsor
beheld the royal knight's approach and summoned
to his aid Kundry, a strange being, who, against her
will, had ever been subservient to his power; and
bidding her practice her arts upon his enemy, he
had little doubt as to the issue.

Nor was he mistaken, for Kundry (who could

assume any shape) transformed herself into a woman of such surpassing beauty that Amfortas felt his senses leave him as he gazed upon her. It was in vain that the young King struggled to maintain his integrity and to fight against the evil influence that closed so surely around him; for Kundry never relaxed her seductions until he was locked in her embrace, in the snares of guilty passion.

Soon, Klingsor, stealing unawares upon his victim, as he lay thus entranced, seized the sacred spear and stabbed him in the side with it; and then, with a triumphant laugh, he rushed back to his Enchanted Castle, bearing the holy relic with him.

The wounded King was carried back by his faithful knights to the Sanctuary, full of remorse for his sin and doomed to suffer agonies of pain for many long, weary years; for the wound inflicted by the evil sorcerer throbbed and burned unceasingly, and could never be healed until the holy spear should be reclaimed and brought back to the Sanctuary, and the unhappy Amfortas remained helpless and agonised in mind and body, with a wound that would not close.

Once, as the King lay groaning in the Sanctuary, the angels of the Holy Grail were heard proclaiming that the sacred spear could alone be regained by " The Blameless Fool," one who, simple and pure, unacquainted with worldly knowledge, should, from pure, whole-hearted sympathy with the sufferer's terrible agony, recognise the woes of suffering humanity, and by such loving pity bring redemption. This, then, was the one hope held out, and the sublime deed to be performed; and, after many long years of woe, the deliverer of Amfortas appeared.

One early dawn, Gurnemanz, one of the oldest of the Grail Knights, was resting with his Esquires in a glade within the sacred domains, waiting for the arrival of Amfortas, who was to be carried, in accordance with his usual daily custom, to bathe in the lake near by, that its soothing waters might ease his ever-burning wound for a short time; and as the first rays of the rising sun shone forth, the solemn morning bell of the Sanctuary was heard calling all to their devotions.

At the sound of the bell, the watchers in the glade knelt reverently to offer up their morning prayer; and as they rose once more to their feet they were joined by other knights.

As the newcomers spoke sadly with old Gurnemanz of the perpetual sufferings of the King, a wild female figure was seen riding furiously towards them; who, upon approaching the knights, flung herself from the foaming steed and hastened to them, bearing in her hand a small crystal vial.

This was none other than Kundry, the witch-maiden, who, when temporarily freed from the evil influence of the sorcerer, Klingsor, would serve the Knights of the Grail as message-bearer, and, by the performance of extraordinary feats of endurance, would seem as though striving to atone by such penances for the evil deeds she did when unable to resist her sinful nature and the commands of her unholy master. She was well-known to the knights, some of whom, however, regarded her with scorn and suspicion, knowing her to be a sinner; but Gurnemanz was always kind and gentle with her, and would often reprove his companions for their hostile attitude, declaring that though she might be under an evil curse, yet she did penance by serving the Grail, and that when she was absent for long, some misfortune was sure to happen to them.

Kundry now appeared as a wild, half-savage crea-ture, clad in a fantastic robe fastened by a girdle of snake-skins, and with long flowing locks of black hair and piercing black eyes, sometimes wildly flash-ing but more usually fixed and glassy; and having travelled far in search of a healing balsam for the wounded King, she handed the vial to Gurnemanz, roughly refusing all thanks.

Amfortas, groaning with pain, now appeared in

the glade in a litter borne by a number of noble knights, and having received Kundry's balsam from Gurnemanz, he thanked her for her gift, although he knew it could afford relief but for a few hours. He was then carried forward to the lake; and soon afterwards—as Gurnemanz remained lost in his sad thoughts, standing beside the now prostrate Kundry, who had flung herself exhausted on the ground—loud cries of indignation were suddenly heard, and as the old knight looked around, he saw a wild swan slowly sink to the ground and die.

At the same moment, the Esquires dragged forth a handsome youth, whose beauty and look of perfect innocence and purity made all regard him with interest and wonder, and yet whose bow and arrows proclaimed him as the slayer of the fair bird, a species held sacred by the Guardians of the Grail.

Gurnemanz poured forth indignant reproaches upon the youth, who, however, appeared unconscious that his deed was wrong; but on seeing the sorrow he had caused, his own heart was touched, and suddenly, breaking his bow and arrows, he impetuously flung them away.

Gurnemanz, struck by the noble looks of the young stranger, began to question him; but the youth declared that he knew not from whence he had come, nor what his name was, nor who his father had been, though he recollected that his mother's name was " Heart-in-Sorrow," and that they had dwelt together in the forest wilds.

Kundry, who, in her weary wanderings over the world, had knowledge of everything, now approached and declared that the stranger's father had fallen in battle, and that his mother had brought him up in a desert place, where he could not learn the use of arms, nor gain any knowledge of the wicked world; and so the lad had led the pure, innocent life of nature, and knew not the meaning of evil. Having beheld a party of knights in glittering armour one day, he had followed them, full of wonder, forgetful of the mother who so tenderly loved him, and whom Kundry now declared had died of grief at his loss.

On hearing this, the youth, feeling for the first time in his life for another than himself, sprang furiously at Kundry's throat, and would have choked her, had not Gurnemanz dragged him back; and then he sank down half-fainting, whilst the witch-maiden hurried to bring water to refresh him.

Gurnemanz, astonished at the utter innocence and primitive simplicity of the handsome stripling, and recollecting the prophecy that one who should be a " Blameless Fool," pure and undefiled, would alone be found worthy to regain the lost spear, regarded the youth with new interest, feeling that the Holy Grail itself must have guided him thither as the one who should indeed perform the supreme deed; and gently laying his hand on the youth's shoulder, he began to tell him about the Holy Grail and its wonderful powers.

Kundry, meanwhile, had crept away unperceived to a thicket, and, overcome by a deadly weariness, sank down into a deep slumber; for this was the means by which Klingsor the sorcerer called her to perform his evil behests, and struggle as she might, she could not prevail against this fatal sleep.

Having explained to the wondering youth the mysterious nourishment and power given by the Holy Grail, the uncovering of which was about to be performed by the King, who had now left the lake and was being carried back to the castle, Gurnemanz took him to join in the sacred ceremony; for he saw plainly that the stranger had noble qualities in him, and believed that these would be stirred into actual being by the holy influence of the Sanctuary treasures.

When they reached the magnificent hall of the Temple, the knights were already assembled, waiting with rapt and reverent attention for the customary unveiling of the Grail, by which they received physical and spiritual food and strength.

The litter of Amfortas was carried forward and placed beside the holy shrine; and then, as all stood round expectantly, the voice of the aged King Titurel was heard from a niche in the background, where he sat in retirement, calling upon his son to uncover the Grail, that its wondrous blessing might yet once more be bestowed upon its guardians.

Amfortas, suffering acutely from the burning and throbbing of his wound, broke forth into agonised lamentation, because he, the most unworthy of them all, should thus be the one whose duty it was to perform this, the holiest office of their order; and in despairing tones, he besought his father to take back his old authority and leave him to die. But the aged King declared he was too feeble to perform the blessed office, and was only kept alive by the daily strength he received from beholding the Grail; and he again commanded Amfortas to proceed with the duties of his position, since by continuing to serve the Grail in spite of his agony, he might atone for his guilt. The knights also reminded their fallen master of the promised deliverance from his woe, and Amfortas, somewhat comforted, raised himself painfully, and, unveiling the Holy Grail, waved it reverently to and fro, thus consecrating the bread and wine, which was then distributed, that all might partake of the wondrous Love-Feast.

As the Holy Cup was revealed, a brilliant light fell upon it, which caused it to glow with a rich wine purple colour, and to shed a soft heavenly effulgence on all around, and Amfortas, though he took no part in the meal, remained for some time in a state of rapt exaltation. Then, as he felt his wound break out afresh, as it ever did when he performed the sacred office, he uttered a long-drawn cry of agony and sank back, fainting and exhausted.

All this time, the strange youth had stood apart, taking no part in the ceremony, but remaining still and dazed, as though entranced; but when the wounded King gave forth his last cry of anguish, he placed his hand with a convulsive movement over his heart, as though filled with an emotion entirely new and strange to him.

But, though pity was thus unconsciously awakened in his breast, he did not yet understand the agonies of a conscious guilt, which was the wounded King's chief woe, nor did he comprehend the meaning of what he had just seen; and Gurnemanz, impatient at such seeming stupidity, and deeming him a fool indeed, irritably thrust him out through a side door of the Temple, bidding him depart to his old wild ways once more, knowing that he must first experience the stabs of passion and temptation in himself, and conquer the same, ere he could understand and feel sympathy for the woes and sins of others.

But the pity that had indeed stirred the youth's heart so strangely for the first time grew apace; and since he had learned from Gurnemanz the story of the lost spear, he determined to try to regain the sacred weapon which alone could give relief to the poor sufferer; and with a fearless spirit and a joyous step, he set off, alone and unafraid, to storm the Enchanted Castle.

Klingsor, the sorcerer, saw him approaching, and at once recognised him as a dangerous foe, since his breastplate was purity, and his shield foolishness; and quickly he called to his aid the witch-maiden, Kundry, whom he had just awakened from the deep slumber of destiny by his magic spells, to work his evil will once more. But though Kundry could not prevail against the terrible power of Klingsor, she only obeyed his commands in anger and horror, doing against her will wicked deeds for which, when removed from her master's influence, she would tearfully endeavour to atone by her acts of mercy and service. She longed above all things to die, but could not; for she who had lived through all the ages, and laughed at everything good and pure, whose spirit had inspired the savage heart of Herodias, and had mocked the Saviour of the world, was now doomed to a path of evil for ever, compelled to lure all into her snares of passion and sin.

On hearing that the simple Fool was to be her victim also, she asked Klingsor in despair if she was never to be released from his toil, and to find rest in eternal sleep; and the sorcerer replied that deliverance for her would only come when someone should be found strong and pure enough to resist her wiles. Kundry, with a heart-rending moan, now resigned herself to the terrible part of temptress she was thus compelled to play, being unable to resist her master's will; and Klingsor, from his magic tower, watched his approaching victim with malignant interest.

As the youth approached the Enchanted Castle with a light step and joyous heart, he found his entry opposed by the fallen knights who had been lured within its walls by Klingsor's beautiful sirens; but, fearlessly resisting them, he snatched a sword from the nearest, and continued boldly to scale the walls, wounding and scattering all who opposed him. For the degraded knights, once so brave and strong, had now grown weak and dull through indulgence, sloth, and voluptuous sin; and the fiery ardour and simple fearlessness of the young invader so daunted these dullards that they soon fled and left him master of the situation.

Having thus triumphed over the weak guardians of the Castle, the handsome stripling gazed proudly around him; and, perceiving the sorcerer's magic garden close at hand, he entered it, marvelling at its luxuriance.

Here he was quickly surrounded by Klingsor's sirens, beautiful flower-maidens, who, clad in gossamer garments, appeared like a throng of brilliant living flowers; and, bewildered and dazzled by the voluptuous beauty of these fair inhabitants of the magic garden, the young man gazed upon them with delight. The sirens, looking upon the handsome stranger as their lawful prey, instantly began to entice him into the snares of passion, each one trying to win him for herself; but the simple youth remained calmly insensible to their soft persuasions, and at last they left him in anger, deeming him to be a Fool, indeed.

Then, suddenly, Kundry appeared, now wearing the form of a maiden more bewitchingly beautiful than any he had yet seen, calling to him in thrilling tones by the name of " Parsifal."

Remembering that this was the name by which his mother had always called him, the youth approached the dazzling vision before him, filled with wonder; and Kundry, after explaining to him that his name meant " Pure-in-Folly," told him again of his mother's love and devotion, and how she had died of grief at his absence from her.

Overcome at the thought of the woe he had caused by his conduct, Parsifal sank weeping to the ground; for this was his first grief, and his first consciousness of his own part in the life of another human being. Kundry, having thus awakened the youth's emotions, now sought by her seductive arts to lure him into the toils of passion; and, offering him the comforts of love, bestowed on him his first lover's kiss.

But at this, Parsifal sprang to his feet, pressing his hand to his heart, for it seemed to him that the wound of Amfortas burned there; and the thought of the wounded King's urgent need recalled his wandering senses to the great mission he had undertaken. In that critical moment, his nature seemed to change, for, in a flash, world-knowledge had come to him, and he realised the great truth of redemption by grace, and understood that he, by conquering temptation, could become worthy of bringing salvation to the stricken King, whose sufferings had awakened sweet pity within his heart.

The temptress never ceased her wily arts for a moment, and the youth felt more and more the pangs of guilty desires and passions burning within him; but when she again encircled him in her sensuous embrace, and pressed a second long kiss upon his

heated brow, he was awakened to the full consciousness of his danger, and repulsed her with horror.
Then, having triumphed over the desires of the flesh,
Parsifal gazed upwards towards the heavens with such
rapt ecstasy upon his face, that Kundry was filled
with remorse, and looked upon him with awe and
wonder; then, fancying she beheld in him the Saviour
of the world, Whom she had mocked as He lay upon
the Cross, she sank at his feet, telling the whole
terrible story of her everlasting sufferings, beseech-
ing him to be pitiful to her and grant her the joy of
being his, if but for one hour only. But Parsifal
sternly replied that he would be condemned ever-
lastingly with her, if even for one hour he forgot his
holy mission.

Finally, as her last effort, the temptress sought to
ensnare him by declaring that her kiss had awakened
in him world-wide knowledge and vision, and that in
her love he might reach unto Godhead and Omni-
potence; but this subtle suggestion Parsifal resisted
also, remaining true to his own pure and noble
nature, and refusing to be enticed from the path of
duty and mercy which he now so clearly recognised.

Then Kundry, finding that all arts and lures were
in vain, sprang furiously from his side, cursing him,
and calling loudly upon her wicked master to avenge
her wrongs; for never before had any man been able
to resist her offers of love.

The sorcerer immediately appeared on the battle-
ments of the Enchanted Castle, bearing aloft the holy
spear; and, casting this with rage at the youth, he
at the same time set forth his evil spells to work
destruction upon his defier.

But his magic was powerless when brought into
contact with purity and faith; and the holy spear
remained hanging in the air over Parsifal's head,
until the noble youth seized it in his hand, and
solemnly made the sign of the Cross with it. Instantly the Enchanted Castle fell to the ground, shaken
by a violent earthquake; the beautiful garden was

changed to a desert once more; and as Kundry sank
to the ground with a cry of woe, Parsifal hastened
from the place of his temptation, triumphantly bearing aloft the sacred spear, with which he was now to
conquer the hostile races of the world.

For many years Parsifal wandered forth alone; and
then at last, when grown to perfect manhood by
suffering and sorrow, he returned to the domains of
the Holy Grail. Here he was gladly welcomed one
morning by the knight, Gurnemanz, now grown to
be a very old man, who had taken up his abode in the
forest, and become a hermit; and he learned from
the old man that most of the Grail Knights had
gradually left the Sanctuary, because Amfortas, in his
agony of body and mind, had refused to perform the
life-preserving office of revealing the Holy Grail,
which had formerly given them such wonderful
nourishment and power. Thus the strength of the
noble knights had dwindled and faded; and the aged
King Titurel had already died, for, deprived of the
nourishment of the Grail, he could no longer live.

On hearing this sad news, Parsifal was overcome
with sorrow, knowing that he had been the cause of
this long-drawn-out woe, because he had for so many
long years neglected to bring the salvation that lay
in his power. But Gurnemanz comforted him, declaring that the suffering King should now be restored, since the only cure for his wound was at last
nigh at hand; and he then invited Parsifal to go with
him to the Sanctuary that day, since it was Good
Friday, and Amfortas was expected to reveal the Holy
Grail once again at the funeral service of the dead
King Titurel.

Whilst the old and the young knight talked thus
together, a female figure had come forth from the
hermit's hut close by, and, drawing slowly nearer,
had stood beside them with bowed head and humble
mien. This was Kundry, who, in her wild witch-
maiden form, Gurnemanz had that morning found in
the forest, wrapped in the usual deep slumber, into

which she had sunk upon being released from the influence of the sorcerer, Klingsor; and, having gently revived her, the good old man had permitted her to perform for him the menial services she ever did at such times. Now approaching Parsifal, she humbly and tenderly washed his feet, anointing them with the contents of a golden vial she drew from her bosom; seeming as though, by such an act of service she would atone for the evil she had formerly tried to work to his soul. Old Gurnemanz then took the vial from her, and poured the remainder of its contents over the head of Parsifal, saluting him afterwards as King and Saviour; and the young knight, filling his hand with water from the sacred spring close by, very gently sprinkled it over the bent head of Kundry, as she knelt at his feet, thus baptising the poor sinner as his first act as the bringer of Salvation.

Gurnemanz now brought forth from the hut the rich scarlet mantle of the Grail Knight, with which he and Kundry proceeded to invest Parsifal over the shining armour which he wore; and then the three very solemnly bent their steps towards the holy castle and entered the Sanctuary.

Here the knights who still remained were gathered beside the bier of the dead King Titurel, waiting for the Holy Grail to be revealed to them; but Amfortas, whose agony was now even greater than ever, and who passionately longed for death, again refused to perform his holy office, and, rising from his litter in a mad frenzy of pain and despair, tore the covering from his wounded side, and wildly implored his faithful companions to plunge their swords into his heart, and thus end his woe.

As the knights drew back in alarm at this outburst, Parsifal stepped forward with noble and calm dignity, and gently touched the suffering King's open wound with the sacred spear that alone had power to cure it; and at the touch of the holy weapon, Amfortas felt his pains vanish, and his wound close, and, knowing that he was now restored and forgiven, he fell upon his knees in an ecstasy of gratitude and praise.

Parsifal now assumed the office of King, which was henceforth his right; and, uncovering the long-unrevealed Holy Grail, he waved it solemnly before the kneeling knights. The Sanctuary was gradually flooded with the dazzling purple light that glowed from the sacred vessel, in the midst of which a white dove was seen to slowly descend from the dome; and as the holy bird hovered over the head of the rapt Parsifal, the witch-maiden, Kundry, sank dying to the ground, at last released from the doom of evil by the noble knight who had been strong enough to resist her wiles.

Thus was the sacred spear restored to the Sanctuary of the Holy Grail, and salvation brought to its guardians by the " Blameless Fool," the true and simple one, whose purity and faith had overcome temptation, and whose awakened pity for the sufferings of others had revealed the real spirit of brotherly love.

.   .   .   .   .   .

It will be plain to all that the story of " Parsifal " is an allegory, and that the incidents and characters of the piece are symbolic of human development, of the conquest of good over evil, and of the revivified spirit soaring triumphant above the baser instincts that struggle to draw it back.

Amfortas represents suffering and guilty humanity. The body of humanity, grievously wounded by the throbbing, burning poison of sin, can only be healed by the restoration of the Genius of Good, which is symbolised by the spear, which has obtained mastery over the powerful spirits of evil. Klingsor represents everything opposed to Goodness and Loving-kindness, being the mainspring and source of all evil. Kundry, the instrument subject to the power of the instigator of ill, signifies the temptations that beset the seeker after Truth—the evil moral law, which the pilgrim can only resist with the strength which is given by purity and faith.   Finally, Parsifal himself is typical of the Saviour of the world, the pure and blameless One, the Conqueror of Temptation, Whose pity and love for wounded, guilty humanity brought salvation to all, and by redemption threw open the way to eternal Life and Love.